The Assam Diaries:

Medicine on a Tropical Tea Estate during the 1950s

CAROLINE ALLANA SCOTT

Copyright © 2025 Caroline Allana Scott

All rights reserved.

ISBN: 9798296807892

DEDICATION

To Allan Scott MBChB DTM&H DObstRCOG

CONTENTS

	Acknowledgments	i
	Introduction	1
1	October to December 1951	8
2	January to March 1952	29
3	April to June 1952	43
4	July to September 1952	61
5	October to December 1952	73
6	January to March 1953	85
7	April to June 1953	97
8	July to September 1953	106
9.	October to December 1953	115
10.	January to March 1954	122
11.	April to June 1954	132
12.	July to September 1954	137
13.	October to December 1954	142
14.	January to July 1955	146
15.	September to December 1955	150
16.	January to December 1956	160
17.	January to December 1957	181
18.	January to May 1958	203
	Afterword and Appendices	212

ACKNOWLEDGEMENTS

Special thanks to my parents for their intrepid travels and for giving me written and photographic material, which has enabled me to write this book. I hope the contents provide fruitful information to assist with future medical developments on tea plantations in Assam and elsewhere in the world.

INTRODUCTION

My father was a medical doctor, spending the final part of his working years in general practice in Kent (England). He did, however, have a very good knowledge of tropical medicine, having lived seven years in Assam (India), caring for the workforces on a number of different tea gardens during the 1950s. But he didn't just treat his patients, he also researched into different methods of malaria control, documenting his findings in published papers and commenting on them in a series of letters he wrote to his parents during his time in India.

Dad began life on 13 March 1924 on Overton Farm, Alexandria, Dunbartonshire (Scotland), the youngest son of a dairy farmer.

Dad aged about three or four, helping his father plough the fields

During his childhood and youth, Dad spent his time working hard at school – as well as involving himself in milking the cows and undertaking other activities on the farm.

Dad with the chickens

In 1941, at the age of seventeen, Dad became a medical student at Glasgow University.

Dad aged 17 years

In 1945, whilst still a student, he was forced to review medicine from a patient's perspective when his mastoid was surgically removed, following an infection. He was admitted to the Ears, Nose and Throat Hospital, St Vincent's Street, Glasgow, where he was introduced to a nurse called Reita (from Islay), who was assigned to look after him – and who later became his wife and my mother.

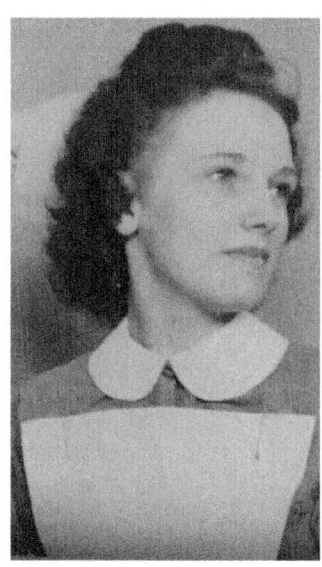

Mum during the 1940s

Dad qualified in 1946, and in 1947 became a resident at the Glasgow Royal Infirmary.

Dad is in the middle row, far right

In 1948, Mum and Dad married...

Wedding Day on 24 March 1948

They moved to Falkirk, where Dad became an assistant general practitioner in a medical practice. In 1951, after three years as an assistant, Dad saw an overseas post, advertised by the tea company Williamson Magor, in the BMJ (British Medical Journal).

They were looking for a principal medical officer, who would be responsible for the welfare of the labour forces (and families) on twelve tea estates, spread out against the Himalayan foothills, north of the Brahmaputra River, in the Assam Valley, North East India.

Each tea garden had its own rudimentary hospital to treat the workers, who were expected to pluck the tea leaves and produce the tea in the factory.

Dad got the job, and in October 1951 he and Mum sailed to India. It was at this time that Dad began to write letters to his parents in Scotland, describing life in Assam.

Dad's Parents

When Dad died in 2004, Mum presented me with a pile of airmail correspondence, which turned out to be the letters to his parents, written between 1951 and 1958. As I read them, I quickly realised just how valuable they were, not only from a medical perspective, but from a geographic, economic and social one.

Mum had never actually read the letters, so when I disclosed the contents to her, she made some very interesting comments. She also drew my attention to a photograph album she had compiled during their time in India, and as I went through it, I realised that not only did Dad's letters provide an account of a bygone era, the photographs, together with Mum's added observations and souvenirs, provided me with an additional resource, allowing me to restore a forgotten part of history and compare it to the present.

This is their story...

Mum and Dad in the 1950s

1

OCTOBER TO DECEMBER 1951

Almost at Gibraltar, 19th October 1951

We went to the Coliseum (London Theatre) and saw a rather uninspiring show and were rather pleased that we could only get 4/- tickets in the gods.

We spent the night at a hotel near Victoria Station (London) so that we could make a quick get-away in the morning.

When we arrived at the docks (Southampton) we spent hours in Customs, but none of our baggage was opened. They do not appear to be very fussy about people leaving the country.

When we boarded the ship (the "Batory") and found our cabin, it was about 3pm, and since we had not eaten, we were starving. The meals on board are lovely. Every sitting has meat, and one can eat as much, as one wishes.

To begin with, the heaving of the boat upset us slightly, but we have got used to it. No one was sick, but quite a few passengers spent Wednesday in bed.

The "Batory": cover of a dinner menu signed by passengers

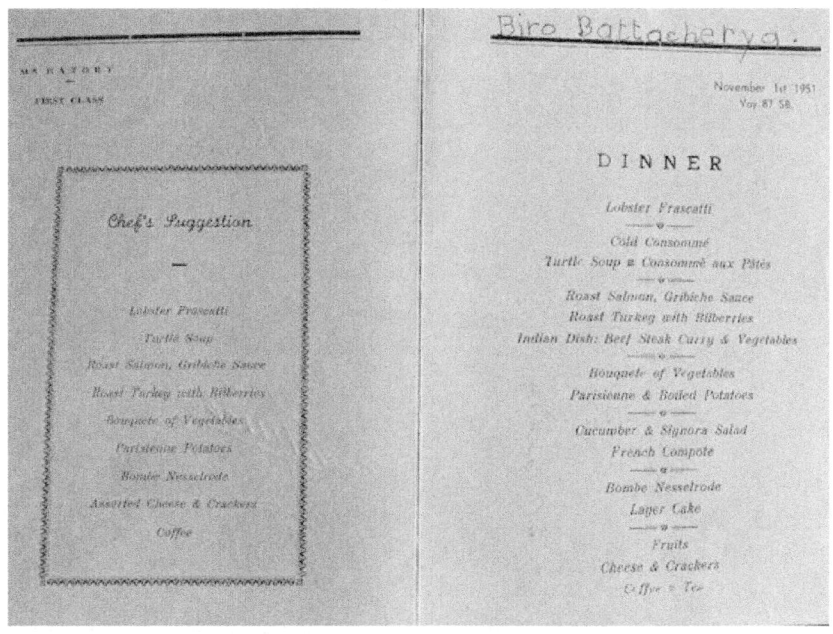

Dinner Menu

We have met quite a few people from Scotland going out to the Tea or Oil in Assam. Our future next-door neighbours – an Edinburgh man: Douglas Taylor (assistant manager) and his English wife, Frances – are on board with us, and they have described our bungalow to us.

Left to right: Frances and Douglas Taylor in Assam

Mum and Dad's Bungalow in Dufflaghur

I am annoyed that I did not bring a shotgun out with me. It appears they are very expensive in India. Despite import duties, it is still more economical to bring a new one over following each leave period. Some people do that, and then sell it in India.

As for wireless sets with suitable wavelengths and protection against tropical dampness, these are also expensive. We will soon find out the best way to deal with such things from personal experience.

Mum

This is the first I've heard about a shotgun! I'm glad he didn't bring one out. What did he want a shotgun for? To shoot his patients?

Anyway, Allan didn't realise the Company (Williamson Magor) was paying for the hotel, and since he could only afford the cheapest, the hotel was dreadful. They brought in a basin of water for us to wash ourselves because there was no running water.

As for Customs, it was as well they didn't open the luggage. I would have been embarrassed. Allan had covered everything with newspapers and sprinkled DDT all over them to keep the insects out. We had such an argument over that. When I eventually opened the luggage, I was nearly asphyxiated.

The food on the ship was great. In Britain we were still using food coupons after the war. When we went to India, the passport controllers took our coupons from us.

As for the "Batory" itself – that was something else. It was a Polish ship, and right from the start I knew something was amiss. Two men with long black coats and funny black hats, carrying attaché cases, were prancing around. I kept asking Allan who they were, and he kept telling me to keep quiet. I still don't know who were the "goodies" and who were the "baddies", but when the ship docked, we discovered it was a communist vessel – and the captain finally jumped ship, never to be seen again.*

***Author's Note**

Nowhere in the letters does it mention that the captain jumped ship, so I did a spot of research and came upon the book: *"The Captain Leaves his Ship – The Story of the Captain of the SS Batory, as told to Hawthorne Daniel"*. This fills in a few gaps and reveals that the captain's name was Jan Cwiklinski, who had been a merchant sea captain at the time of the Second World War. Initially involved in the transport of arms to Britain and the conveyance of refugees to safety, he was then sent to Holland, in 1940, to pick up a new ship: *"Warszawa II"*, which belonged to the Polish-British Steamship Line. Unfortunately, whilst in Holland, the Nazis, who had already taken Poland, claimed ownership of the Line, and matters were delayed. When the Nazis occupied Holland, Cwiklinski found himself stranded in Amsterdam, dependent on financial hand-outs from the Dutch Red Cross. He remained stuck there, a refugee, for five years.

After the war, Fascism was of course replaced by Communism. Cwiklinski, who was a Roman Catholic, tried to continue peacefully with his job as captain of the "Batory", but over the years, as his crew changed, the ship became manned by a majority of communists, who spied on Cwiklinski and fabricated reports about him. These reports were sent to the Polish Secret Police, rendering Cwiklinski a target for political assassination. In the Spring of 1953, when the "Batory" was undergoing repairs in Newcastle (England), Cwiklinski was warned by a crew member that his life was in danger. So, to avoid political assassination, he simply walked off the ship, and was finally granted political asylum in America, where he circulated the story of communist oppression in Poland, until his death in 1976.

Near Port Said, 23rd October 1951

We have been enjoying our trip along the Mediterranean very much indeed, and have dispensed with superfluous clothing.

Mum and Dad on the "Batory"

    I do not think we will have any bother at the Canal (Suez Canal: anti-British unrest) despite the "News". The system of getting news on the ship is very poor. We do not get the BBC Bulletins, and we have to rely on a daily type-written sheet that is pinned on the notice board.

    We met one of the representatives from the BDH (British Drug House). His name is Eden Rollo. He was with his wife, Agnes, and both are travelling to Bombay. They are from North Berwick.

Left to right: Mum, Eden and Agnes Rollo

Left to right: Mum, Dad and Agnes Rollo

Our evenings on the ship are filled with either films or dancing. Tonight, we have the film: "Grounds for Marriage". The films, in the main, have been quite enjoyable.

Socialising on the "Batory"
Dad and Mum: middle
Eden and Agnes: third (standing) and second (sitting) from right

When we arrived at Gibraltar, the few passengers who were disembarking and embarking, were taken in a small boat, and we were not allowed to go ashore. The number of passengers and goods did not warrant a delay.

Approaching Gibraltar: Mum

The local boys from the nearby Spanish town were soon out in their small boats, selling their wares. It was quite amusing watching them throw a line up to the deck, and passing stuff up in a basket. Unfortunately, there was really very little worth buying.

Mum

I remember Eden and Agnes. We were in touch for a long time. On the boat, we used to drink beer on deck.

Drinking Beer: Agnes, Eden and Mum

Near Aden, 28th October 1951

Since we wrote last, we have covered quite a bit of territory. When we were approaching the Canal (Suez Canal), we felt quite tense, despite all the reassurances.

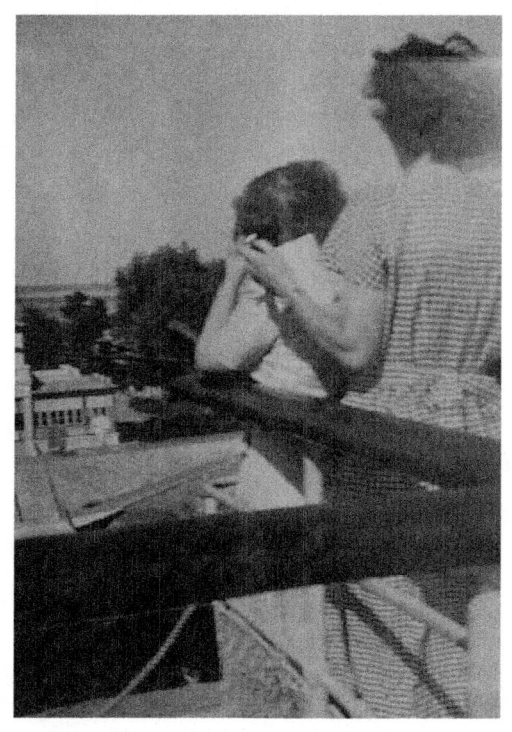

Mum and Agnes at the Suez Canal

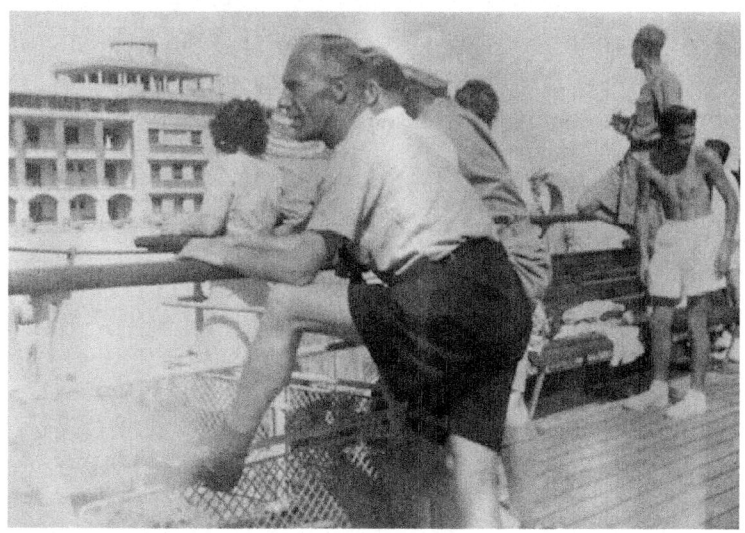

Other passengers at the Suez Canal

The first indication of Egypt was the appearance of tall palm trees on the beach. When we were still well out, the ships that had been going through the Mediterranean began to converge, and a small vessel with an Egyptian pilot on board came alongside. It was not long until we were right in Port Said. It was a lovely sight. We were not allowed to disembark, and our captain and an Egyptian police officer had a few heated words of conversation. The captain did not wish anyone to go ashore, and the officer did.

The small boats with their wares soon arrived round the ship, and we eventually bought two cotton sun hats for 2/- each.

We waited until the ship entered the Canal at 2am. The Canal has to work twenty-four hours per day to keep the shipping from gathering. The pilots on the Canal are French, and there must be quite a French community for an Egyptian came on board with French newspapers.

Suez was lovely. There were large searchlights, and a loud French voice from a loudspeaker directed the tugs, who then left us, allowing us to make a slow, steady run through the Canal with desert on either side, and on through the bitter lakes. There were miles and miles of desert with green patches of irrigation, and there was also the inspiring sight of our "boys" in uniform all the way down in clusters. Banter was exchanged between the soldiers and the passengers. Unfortunately, the Red Sea has been very uncomfortable, and the least exertion makes us pour with perspiration.

Mum

Well, one week later, the Canal was badly affected by serious fighting between British soldiers and the Egyptians. The British had already left the rest of Egypt, but still occupied Suez, and wanted to maintain control of it for trade. Something to do with an easier route to the East. But the Nationalists wanted them out. We were very lucky to miss the conflict – we learned that it was very bloody.

Near Bombay, 3rd November 1951

We landed in Aden on Monday, and had quite a time going round the shops.

Mum, Eden and Agnes approaching Aden

There is no purchase tax there, and if you can beat them down in price, you can get a good bargain. Reita got a watch (a Rolex Oyster), which cost £13, but there was not sufficient time to make full use of the cheap shopping. The streets were full of beggars, and we were quite pleased to get back to the ship.

I have since discovered that to obtain a driving licence in India without a test, I will have to show my British licence. This was the last thing I was expecting to require. I'd be obliged if you could send it on to me by airmail. Put it in a strong envelope, and ask the Post Office to airmail it to Dufflaghur Tea Estate. I will get a licence issued in Assam when it arrives. Since I will have a driver, anyway, it will not matter too much if there is a slight delay.

Mum

I was embarrassed when Allan was haggling in the shops. I kept telling him to be quiet, and he was telling me to shut up. I didn't realise that everyone did it.

It was one of the passengers who told me to look for a Rolex watch, and all the women said I had to get Chanel No. 5.

Dufflaghur Tea Estate, 16th November 1951

When we arrived at Bombay, we got on a train to Calcutta and began a very dreary journey across India. The train was dirty and dusty, and there were no beds. We had to sit all the time. People were travelling on the roof and hanging on to the sides of the train, for which reason, there were iron bars across the glassless windows. Beggars sat on the edge of the rail. When we got to Calcutta at 11.30am on Tuesday, we were very dirty indeed.

The countryside in Central India is very desolate, and the rice crop is very poor. To look at rice it seems almost like wheat, but when we came up to the fertile countryside of Assam, we saw lovely crops. We stayed a few days in Calcutta, and had quite a list of shopping to do: wireless set, stores and more light clothing, and at the same time, I had to nip round all the firms (Tea) and have a chat with the different people. We stayed at the Grand Hotel, and the Company (Williamson Magor) covered the bill.

We left Calcutta on the Friday (by air) and arrived at our final destination (Dufflaghur Tea Estate) on Sunday. We are staying with the assistant manager (Douglas Taylor) and have been kindly received. We are moving into our bungalow tomorrow.

I have received the driving licence, and have dispatched it to Tezpur (our local administrative town) with an application form, which is more or less a copy of the British one. This will save me travelling eighty-five miles for a driving test.

Mum

It wasn't just Williamson Magor who employed Allan. There were other tea companies, which he refers to as firms, including McLeod Russel, but I didn't really pay attention to the structure of things at the time.

Douglas Taylor (the assistant manager) and his wife, Frances, were with us on the train, travelling to Calcutta. It was a dreadful journey which lasted several days and nights, and I had a splitting headache. The Grand Hotel, however, was lovely, apart from the rats dancing around the entrance.

I remember flying from Calcutta, and I seem to recall that we were late in arriving and had to stay with a friend of Douglas' for the night, before crossing the river to begin the journey to Dufflaghur. That was my introduction to ants. They were everywhere, and I couldn't eat my dinner.

Dufflaghur Tea Estate, 28th November 1951

We have settled into our bungalow. The roof is of corrugated iron, painted with highly-reflective aluminium paint to reflect the heat. The only alternative is thatch, but owing to the danger of fire, I prefer it as it is. A bungalow in the district with a thatched roof was completely gutted owing to fire.

Front of the bungalow

Rear of the bungalow

Dad on the veranda

We have not yet received the wooden box with our household effects. One airline would not accept it on the freight plane, and Cooks are trying to get it up on another line, which calls at Pakistan (East) on the way. I had to send an inventory back to Calcutta for Customs declaration before it would be accepted, and at the moment I do not know whether it is on its way or not. However, we are striving on, borrowing this, that and the other.

The wireless we bought in Calcutta has been installed, and we are able to get the "News". Short wave listening is not terribly satisfactory, and we have not yet discovered the various wavelengths, which change at different times. We do, however, get the "BBC News", or Australian, or American. I think the American is relayed from Ceylon. The "All-India Programme" is not much use owing to the language, although they have short programmes in English. We also get "Radio Moscow" very easily, and they give five minutes propaganda in English, repeating it all afternoon.

We are managing to organise our servants a bit better now. We had great difficulty at first, not knowing a word that was being said. The gardeners have abandoned the plants in the back garden, and I have not had much time to do anything with them so far.

We had thunder and lightning last night, with a downpour of rain. Today, however, it is absolutely dry again, although rather cold. We now require a fire in the evening. It is unusual to get rain in any quantity in November.

We had a leopard in the tea garden a few days ago. Someone had stolen its cubs and taken them to a neighbouring tea garden, and the mother returned to our tea garden during the day (unusual), looking for them. The workforce on our garden had to be organised into "beaters". They stood in a long row and shouted at the pitch of their voices. The assistant manager (Douglas Taylor) was at the ready with the manager's rifle. About twenty yards ahead, the leopard moved slowly from cover to cover, through the tea bushes. Douglas aimed and fired, but there was only a "click". The bullet was correct in bore, but it was the wrong make, and it had slipped down the breech. The leopard got away and has been wandering around the bungalows every night since then. They are repairing the trap (like a rat trap with sliding heavy steel doors), and will put the cubs inside as bait.

I got an urgent call to a neighbouring tea garden (yesterday) to see one of the workers. It was a man who had been mauled by a bear. It would appear the bear had come into the tea garden from the jungle during the night, and had fallen asleep among the tea bushes. He was literally scalped, and one of his eyes and half of his face had been knocked away. He died this morning.

We are eating well. The meat is mostly goat flesh, which is quite nice, but a bit monotonous. Douglas is getting us banana cuttings for our back garden, and to keep fit, we are hoping to play a bit of tennis. We bought two tennis rackets (Rs 30/-/- each).

Tennis Court at Dufflaghur

Mum

Well, I certainly didn't play – and he didn't keep it up! I can't remember what happened to the tennis rackets, but I used to play cards for money – and I always won. I remember the leopard looking for her cubs. I don't know who took the cubs in the first place, and I don't recall what happened. What I do remember is that the leopard would usually come out during the night, and the sound they made was like wood being sawn.

Dufflaghur Tea Estate, 9th December 1951

Our location is interesting. The foothills of the Himalayas are only three quarters of a mile from our bungalow, and from there, they retreat in ridges of ever-increasing height, until their large peaks (snow-covered) can be seen in the distance. The lower ridges and valleys are covered by jungle and abound with wildlife.

We had a rogue female elephant a few weeks ago. She had become separated from the herd and came down early and trampled down the growing paddy (rice), doing a lot of damage to the crop. Food is very scarce for the workforce, and they are dependent wholly on the rice crop.

There is a ban on elephant shooting, and special permission to shoot the female rogue had to be obtained from the Assam Provincial Government. One of the keen sportsmen was allocated the task. He was eager to get the rogue because this would give him the "go-ahead" to shoot a "tusker" (male) that had been knocking down mud huts by the river, and allow him to keep the tusks. According to a special order, the Government gets the tusks, unless a female is shot within a short time of killing a male. Something to do with the balance of nature. Unfortunately, when he followed the female two miles into the jungle, he was unable to get a proper shot, and it is dangerous to shoot if you cannot definitely kill. The female disappeared, and has never been seen since – much to the annoyance of the sportsman.

Not much more to say about the animal life, except I saw one of the few monkeys in this district, last week. We are eating well (no beef of course), but food is quite expensive.

Reita has ordered material from Calcutta for curtains and clothes for the servants, which we hope will arrive quite soon. We received our wooden box on Friday, and it was quite a relief to know it was safe. The bungalow looks nicer with our own odds and ends in place. However, when we opened the box, we found all our coffee saucers and the tea set bowl had smashed. We consider ourselves lucky, nevertheless.

The weather is very nice just now. We are going about in shorts all day long (despite there being only sixteen days to Christmas), but the evenings are cool when the sun goes down. Reita is handling the servants better, despite the language barrier. It's amazing what you can do with only two words of Hindi. Lastly, I operated today, and removed two pints of pus from a liver abscess.

Mum

I don't know why we didn't take photos of the inside of the bungalow. We'd a very big sitting room with a stone coal fireplace. I used cardinal polish to make it red. We had a Jute carpet (reddish) and cream-coloured emulsioned walls. We had a three-piece green suite, occasional chairs and bits and pieces.

The bedroom was huge with mesh on the windows to keep the mosquitoes out. No curtains to begin with, but over the years, I bought different coloured curtain material to match the different carpets. There was a chest of drawers, wardrobe, dressing table and two single beds. A dressing room was off the bedroom, which I let Allan use. I remember finding eggs there one day, and asking the cook what they were. One of the bearers tried to tell me a mouse had laid them. The cook gave him such a mouthful! They were lizard eggs. I was frightened of the lizards to begin with, but got used to them after a while because they ate the insects. You would see a handful of them scurrying up the walls.

Then there was the spare room. It was similar to ours, but instead of mesh on the windows, the beds were inside a big cage. All the other windows in the house had wire mesh.

The bathroom was off the dressing room, down a couple of steps. To begin with we didn't have running water. The Pani Wallah carried the water from the well in big kerosene tins. Eventually we got cold running water, which was dark brown and had to be boiled for our baths. There was a toilet and wash hand basin as well.

The dining room had a huge table. There was a sideboard and side tables. The fridge was kept there. It ran on kerosene. We ran our own generator for electricity, but there was no gas. We kept boiled water in the fridge. There was a small kitchen off the dining room, where a steriliser was kept. The cooking was done in the cookhouse, which was a separate building. And of course, there was the veranda with garden-type furniture.

Then there was Allan's office. He had a desk and an old-fashioned typewriter, which he used with one finger. There was also a small laboratory off the office, where Allan kept his bits and pieces. There was a box with home-made shelves for his files. I remember one day he could hear a noise coming from it, and he told me he thought it was a rat. Well, I was out the bungalow in a jiffy, and ran down the road to the manager's bungalow, leaving Allan to deal with it. He told me later that he shone his torch into the box, and a pair of eyes stared back. It was a rat and her babies...

Dufflaghur Tea Estate, 22nd December 1951

The weather here is just lovely. We have had no rain for a couple of weeks, and everything is becoming very dry and dusty, especially the roads, which have no proper tarmac surface. When rain comes during the cold season, it never really amounts to much. During the day, it is quite cold in the bungalow. We keep all the windows and doors open, and have to go out on the lawn to get a heat!

We have started playing tennis. Our standard could not be called the best, but at least it gives us exercise and keeps us in good trim. We have been invited by the manager (Mr Russell) from the neighbouring tea garden (Boroi) to go up river (some of it is in the jungle) and have a picnic lunch. There appears to be quite a crowd from all the neighbouring tea gardens going there on Christmas Day. Some fish, some swim and others just enjoy the fresh air.

There have been no more animal encounters, although when we recounted our experiences to-date to another medical officer's wife, she said she had been in Assam for three years and had seen nothing. Their practice, however, is more in the open, whereas we are right up against the hills and jungle.

We had a day's outing to the big town last Saturday, to do some shopping. Tezpur is about eighty-five miles away. The place is not just the best of beauty; however, I've no doubt it compares favourably with other parts. The houses, which are mostly mud and bamboo, with the occasional corrugated iron roof, are all crowded together, and the streets are full of people, cows, goats, bullock carts and (occasionally) ducks. In Calcutta, the streets have an abundance of beggars and cripples in addition, but the roads there are surfaced, and the policeman at the corner directs this very varied intermingling of traffic.

The taxis in Calcutta are all large American saloons (none in Tezpur), bought from the Yankees at the end of the war. This whole area was very active during the war. Supplies that were sent to China were flown over from India. In Assam, there was an aerodrome every fifty miles or so to catch any planes in distress coming back after crossing the mountains.

All the troops retreating from Burma (Myanmar) were rescued in Lower Assam in an exhausted condition, after breaking through miles and miles of jungle. Before self-rule (1947), all the tea planters (managers, etc) were in the Volunteers, and they did a great deal of work during the war. They would take their labour force away for months at a time into advanced jungle fronts, and build aerodromes and bridges. There is now a small company plane, thirty-five miles away (in Bishnauth), which is available for any emergency medical work.

We have procured a new sitting room suite, which is very nice, and the only other thing to report is one small quake, which we slept through during the night.

2

JANUARY TO MARCH 1952

Dufflaghur Tea Estate, 8th January 1952

We had quite a quiet time at Christmas and New Year. In this country the younger ones go to the different club parties within a radius of sixty miles, but that would have been too much of an ordeal with so many introductions. We confined ourselves to our own local club (Halem), where we are getting to know all the folks. We went to a grand dance and party at Hogmanay. This is the annual event here, and our club supplied the visitors for miles around with a nice fish supper (in paper) about 10pm. At midnight, a mock pipe band with paper kilts and all the frills appeared, and to our astonishment, we found it was composed of most of the Englishmen in the district, who by the way, are in the minority.

On Christmas Day we had a picnic lunch by the river (Boroi) in the jungle. When we arrived, there was quite a contingent there. The spot is only just accessible by car, and we landed in a big valley behind the first lot of hills, about seven miles from Dufflaghur. The Government gives the local tea gardens a small grant to keep this road open. Just beyond this area is political territory, and a special permit is required to go there. The water, fresh from the jungle, is clear and unpolluted, and we had a great swim, sunbathed and ate good food. The manager (Mr Russell: an Aberdonian known as

"Smiler") from Boroi Tea Garden, who invited us, had converted one of the small boats, composed of wooden spars and tarpaulin, into quite a good effort with kerosene tins (the ones used to boil up bath water) sealed at the seams. We dotted about on this glorified banana skin, on and off, all day, and thoroughly enjoyed ourselves.

Left to right: Smiler, his son, Angus, and wife, Bridget (Russell)

Left to right: Frances Taylor, Mum, Dad, Douglas Taylor, Bridget Russell and Angus

We had a visit from Mr Brett, one of the superintendents (Williamson Magor), who had travelled out on the ship with us. He has been promoted to the Calcutta office. He arrived in a small company plane from Bishnauth, which swooped over the bungalow, before landing on our strip, and after landing at the other end, it taxied round to the side of my garage. I was quite surprised to see it, figuratively speaking, coming up the garden path.

Airfield behind the Bungalow: Mum is in the centre of the photo

Mr Brett had come to see if we were settling in and to discuss any problems we might have. He also advised that the neighbouring doctor (in Bishnauth) is leaving in March, and suggested the possibility of us going there to run the two practices together. He told Reita, who has just received her curtain material, to refrain from having it made up at the moment, in case we do move.

Mum

Bloody nuisance! I remember when Mr Brett came, I wanted to keep my trousers on, but Allan said that would be disrespectful, so I had to wear a skirt.

I do remember "Smiler". He was always smiling. He and his wife, Bridget, who was English, had a small boy, Angus, who hadn't started school.

As for Christmas and the New Year – they were far from quiet! But Allan wouldn't want to tell his parents that! It was always very jolly with Scottish music. Everyone had records and there was singing, dancing and drinking. Someone played the bagpipes. I remember the fish supper. I don't know what the fish was. It was in batter, but there was no taste. I can't remember the chips, but out there the cooks could do anything.

Dufflaghur Tea Estate, 21st January 1952

We are able to follow the "World News" on the wireless since we have mastered the various stations and times. Indian standard time is five and a half hours ahead, and we in the tea gardens are a further hour ahead to get the extra time at night.

The bridge between the two parts of my practice will be due to be washed away in another month, when the increasing heat liquefies the snow on the mountains.

In answer to Pop's question, the woman with the liver abscess is doing very well. I opened it between the lower ribs on the right-hand side, and left a rubber drainage tube in position, which drained large amounts of pus for about a fortnight. Unfortunately, the flesh just fell from her and I thought she was not going to make it, but eventually I got the infection killed, and the wound is now healed and she is being built up.

How did Pop like going to the barber? My barber comes to the bungalow and scalps me when required. Sorry about my handwriting. I have a typewriter, but it takes me too long to type with one finger.

Our tea garden occupies one thousand acres, of which about six hundred are under tea. It is only a moderate size garden. The tea is planted out, and the bushes take about four to five years before they are worth very much. Scattered among the bushes are shade trees, which vary in size according to the whim of the agency. These, in addition to providing shade, "fix" nitrogen from the air (like the bean), and the leaves provide excellent manure as they fall. The tea, which does so well in the very moist heat, away from the full strength of the sun, is plucked during the hot weather when the growth is active.

The best tea, however, is at the beginning and end of the season (slower growth). From the field, it is laid out in large storeyed "leaf houses" to dry, and after reaching a definite stage (about ten days), is put through rollers to burst the individual cells of the leaf, without tearing the leaf (as little as possible, anyway), so that oxidation can take place within the cells. It is then toasted, packed and sent to London, where it is sold in bulk and usually blended after that.

Mum looking out at the tea

I am glad your hens are laying well. We are quite well off for eggs too, but the Indian egg is much smaller than at home. It is slightly bigger than that of a bantam. As for the hen, it can fly into the trees at a moment's notice. There is also wild fowl for shooting, and I am really sorry I did not bring a gun out with me. A very indifferent gun out here costs a minimum of £90, and guns can only be brought into the country if accompanied personally.

Mum

That bloody gun I knew nothing about...

Dufflaghur Tea Estate, 9th February 1952

I have received word from Calcutta to say that a new doctor is being flown out in April to take over the other practice (Bishnauth), so we will not have to move. They have probably concluded that there is not much to be gained by switching over, when my tropical experience will only be a few months ahead of the new man's – or possibly, the new man already has some tropical experience. In any case, they have asked me to carry on the two practices until his arrival.

The neighbouring club (Halem) had their annual sports meeting (tennis and golf) last Sunday, with a dance in the evening. We did not go during the day, but went along to the dance at night. We had a great time, but unfortunately, the couple that came with us and guided us had to leave early to attend to their baby, and on the way back, we took the wrong road. We drove for one hundred and fifty yards, and came to a signpost which said: "Tezpur", one way, and "Old Behali", the other. It was then I realised we were on the wrong road, but I turned along the "Old Behali" road, as I knew this would take us back to the main road without turning back.

In this part of the world there are many little wooden bridges over deep ruts in the road that drain away the rain water during the monsoon, and when they take the bridges down to renew them, they do not always put up a sign or road block. In short, when the full significance of a particular rut in the road (about four feet broad by two feet deep) became obvious in the headlamps, it was too late to prevent ourselves going in with a bump.

There was, fortunately, very little damage to the car (bent steering rod and lost front number plate), but Reita bumped her head on the dashboard. I do not know how the car managed to get out, but it did so under its own steam. We were later told that we had got off lightly in gaining experience of the Indian roads, but I felt it rather badly, having so recently arrived and given the car a bump. After a few days

Reita felt fine.

Although we settled in very nicely to begin with, the stage of reaction has set in, and at the moment, neither of us could truly say that we are settled. Everything is so different; however, I presume that we are going through the normal human reactions, which will pass off again quite soon.

We have not had long enough to observe the wildlife, and will probably have to get a book to properly appreciate what we are looking for. There are no rabbits, but plenty of hares, which raid the vegetable garden. I have seen a few ponies, but the cow and buffalo are the beasts of burden. A herd of cattle looks very big, until you realise that half of them are bulls. The amount of milk given by a cow is very much less than that given by a cow at home, as the animal is only three-quarters the size. Wild dogs prowl round at night, and the wildest is a huge thing with black stripes. We have not heard of any more leopards in the district.

The apple tree will not grow in Assam, as it gets confused with the seasons. The winter would suit it fine, but the monsoon kills it. All the vegetables grown at home do well out here in the winter, but die quickly, if planted during the rains (summer months).

The tea tree is kept very small by constant pruning. They allow it to grow a few inches for a few years, until it reaches twenty-eight inches, and then they cut it down to twenty-four inches again. The women do the pruning and the plucking. They are given their correct level, and cut everything away at that height.

At the moment, I am trying to catch up with the Government's regulations regarding the welfare of the labour force and the requirements of the Government regarding facilities which should be provided, and on which, I have to keep the managers informed. All these regulations were passed during the war years, and are now being brought into force.

We have had stores and cigarettes sent up to do us over the monsoon. The cigarettes out here are all made in India. They are not very good, but much cheaper. Capstans cost Rs 3/2 per tin of fifty; Players cost Rs 3/4; and Virginia No. 10, which we smoke, costs Rs 1/8 per tin. I do not believe, however, that they have ever been near the State of Virginia, but they are no worse than the more expensive ones.

We were sorry to hear about the King's sudden death. Even in India, the post office closed for a day of mourning.

Mum

I bumped my head against the dashboard?!! I don't think so! My head went through the windscreen! I had lumps of glass in my forehead for days, and my head was sore! I seem to remember that another tea planter was with us, and the reason the car started again, was because he and Allan peed on something under the bonnet – so never mind the car starting "under its own steam", they were the ones "creating steam..."

The King, of course, was George VI, and when he died, I remember turning the wireless on, and there was silence. We didn't understand what was going on, and it wasn't until later that evening that we found out the King had died.

Dufflaghur Tea Estate, 24th February 1952

We had a tailor (dursi) in doing our curtains this week, and he has kept us occupied. In all, we have one hundred and two yards of curtain material, which is forty-eight inches broad. The total cost of material, tape, thread, curtain rings and tailoring, works out about £35, or slightly more. Furthermore, the Company has decided to give us a writing bureau, filing cabinet and a further wardrobe, so we are becoming nicely furnished.

I am preparing the annual reports for the individual tea gardens just now, and this being my first time, and having to rely on the records, I am finding it time-consuming. Nevertheless, I went up river for a few hours today (Boroi) with a neighbour and his wife, and had a nice swim and sunbathe. Reita did not come. She occupied herself with the tailor and the curtains.

I will be travelling down to the neighbouring practice (Bishnauth) every day this week, except Monday, to become familiar with it before the doctor goes home. I cannot go on Monday, as I have a spleen muster in my own area in the morning. The spleen index of the children on a tea garden gives a good idea of the incidence of malaria, and I have been doing these and anaemic musters, early every morning for the past month.

Spleen Muster: Dad would screen the workforce and their families for malaria parasites, looking for clinical symptoms such as fever, chills, headaches and body aches. An enlarged spleen in a child would indicate malaria.

Dad examining eyes in adults for signs of malaria – also iron deficiency.

Paludrine has brought the number of spleens down from 40-60% to 5-15%. A normal haemoglobin (red pigment) out here is 60%, as the diet of the labour force is so deficient in protein (not eating meat – and milk, eggs and fish are expensive for them). I have patients with haemoglobin 25%, and although at home this would cause terrific consternation, out here it is quite the routine thing.

Some of the hospitals here are very nice with reasonable facilities and equipment. Most are not just the best as far as cleanliness goes, and patients have to lie on the floor; but it is amazing what one is able to do in the better-equipped ones. Washing is not a priority, and you find the women beating their clothes on stones in the river to clean them. This is their only way, as soap in any quantity is well out of their budget. When a worker becomes ill, he reports to the hospital, and if necessary, is admitted. The relatives who come in to make food and attend to sanitary arrangements, do the nursing of the patient.

Washing clothes in the river

One gets a great array of clinical material out here that would never be seen in such a short time at home. This week has been one of fractures, the great majority of which, we treat on the tea garden, unless they prove to be difficult or complicated.

They are very fond of cock fighting out here, and one man in the hospital had sustained an injury to one of the arteries of his leg (aneurysm) from a deep stab of one of the artificial spurs, which they put on the cock's legs. As it was nearly at bursting point when I saw him, I decided to operate and tie off the blood vessel. We got him on the table, and with the tourniquet ready to apply, I injected the area with local anaesthetic; I was enlarging the wound, when the aneurysm burst with a spray of blood which drenched me. Fortunately, it was an easy matter to apply the tourniquet and finish the job. He did very well.

Mum

The dursi, like the cook, was wonderful. I think they were all self-taught, and they could do anything. You would give the dursi an existing dress, and he could make an identical one. In fact, someone once told me they gave him an item of clothing with a patch – and he reproduced the patch!

Dufflaghur Tea Estate, 13th March 1952

The doctor in the neighbouring practice has now left for home. He went away on Tuesday, and is due to sail from Bombay on 19th March.

Most of the medical regulations in this part of the world are the fulfilment of acts of Government. They make it compulsory for the Tea Industry to provide various services to the labour forces: medical, holidays, fasting, etc, more or less as at home. Although these acts were passed before and during the war, it is only now that full pressure is being made to bear on these problems. The import duty on any article of machinery, which would save manpower, is prohibitive, so there will always be work available. The food problem for the worker is very great, and in order to be able to keep a labour force, the tea garden buys rice, etc, and sells it to them at a loss. Since the rice shortage, wheat products have been substituted, much to the consternation of the workers, and the Government started an allocation scheme so that everyone would have a fair ration. Unfortunately, they were not always able to have rice to allocate, and it was very difficult to explain this to the labour force.

It is very interesting to be out here and see the ways of the people. The bird life and plant life offer plenty of scope, but I have enough on my hands at the moment, learning the language and adapting myself. After a year, when I've caught up with everything, I think life should prove more interesting and relaxing. Last weekend, we had a thunderstorm with a downpour of rain. The roads, which are mostly shingle or hard-packed earth, became very muddy and difficult to negotiate. The wooden bridges are all being repaired just now, and detours have to be made round them over ground that is usually almost dry. Unfortunately, the ground on the detours was not packed hard, and after the rain, became so muddy that even the Land Rover had the greatest of difficulty in managing along. On one such day, the road was completely blocked up by a bogged-up lorry on one side, and a bus on the other. I had to turn back and work on a nearer tea garden that day. The next day, however, I did manage to get through.

Dad and the Land Rover

The drains through the tea gardens are cut very deep and steep, in order to be able to cope with the terrific rush of water during the monsoon. We are very unlikely to be much affected by major flooding, being so near the foothills. It is in the central plains that the danger occurs mostly.

We have had one or two small tremors since we arrived. I have not felt any of them, having either been asleep or outside. Reita felt them in the bungalow, and the fans began to sway quite a bit.

The thunderstorm, last weekend, seems to be unusual for the time of year, and they were attributing this to the very scanty amount of rain we had at Christmas. It is very obvious when there is going to be rain. The clouds gather for quite a few days beforehand, and it becomes duller and duller, until the lightning starts. The storm is now well away, and the roads are almost as dry as ever. It becomes very pleasant for a few days after the rain to have no clouds of dust flying along the roads with you. The weather is beginning to get warmer, but it is still very pleasant.

Mum

I seem to recall it was very windy in March. Dust would fly everywhere, and your hair would be saturated in it. I remember the tremors. The overhead fans would swing back and forth – although we didn't call them fans. We called them punkahs. There was never anything serious, but I used to get frightened in case the ground opened up and swallowed me!

Dufflaghur Tea Estate, 17th March 1952

I have had quite a hectic time since I started this letter on 13th March. Firstly, I had to complete a medical examination of a new member of staff, following concerns raised by other staff members. He, unfortunately, had not been properly vetted, and was not terribly good from a psychiatric point of view.

Next, I got a call to the other end of the district (thirty-five or forty miles away) in the early hours of Saturday morning, and had to return again during the day. This was to deal with a European case of tuberculosis. The patient was at that time in rather a weak state, owing to haemoptysis (coughing of blood). I am hoping to get her to Calcutta or Shillong this week.

Then, last night, I had another night call in my own district to see the wife of one of the Indian staff, who was suffering from acute intestinal obstruction due to adhesions from a previous intra-abdominal suppurative condition, for which I treated her about three weeks ago. She delivered unto herself a son at that time, with peritonitis at the same time. She would not go into hospital, but did quite well with Sulphonamides, Penicillin and Chloromycetin, until this obstruction developed.

Lastly, I had a suspected case of smallpox today. The rash is not completely out yet, but we will see what it definitely is by tomorrow. I have got one of the AMOs (assistant medical officers) busy vaccinating all the contacts, to be on the safe side. There are usually a few cases now and then, but this will be my first, if it does happen to be one.

Sending a patient to one of the big hospitals (mission hospitals) means around twelve hours on the night steamer, up and across the river. The Europeans have the privilege of taking the small plane, which is becoming very popular on the tea gardens in Assam. They are cheaper than the expensive cars, working out about £1,000; but unless the manager has an expert knowledge of the servicing, he is taking quite a risk. The normal flying hours of one of these planes works out at a little over ten each week.

3

APRIL TO JUNE 1952

Dufflaghur Tea Estate, 8th April 1952

We are getting very much better reception from the BBC now. At first, it was variable, but I do try to make a point of hearing the "News" every day. I was, however, unfortunate in not hearing the budget details on the wireless, and am looking forward to seeing them in the newspapers you send, quite soon.

We are beginning to feel the heat now. It was funny to think that you were having snow so recently. We have stopped having fires in the evening, and from last weekend, we have started the fans very gently, to keep a breeze going. It will not be very long until the real heat begins and the monsoon breaks. We have got into the habit of having a short lie-down in the afternoon, and after trotting about in and out of the sun until 1, 2 or 3pm, I am always ready for it and much refreshed by it.

The new doctor (Arthur Chesshire) arrived in the neighbouring practice yesterday (Bishnauth). Apparently, he left medicine during the war to join the RAF and was a bomber pilot, after which, he resumed his studies and qualified. I am in no doubt that they are thinking it will be very useful to have his flying experience when there are now two small planes on the other side of the river. His wife (Daphne – also a doctor) and small child (Sarah) of five months are still at home and will come out later, after the monsoon.

Arthur Chesshire

Left to right: Daphne Chesshire and Mum

Baby Sarah

Dufflaghur Tea Estate, 12th April 1952

I had intended going over to visit the new doctor, and arrange to show him round next week, but he came to see us on Wednesday. I thought that would save me a trip to Bishnauth, but I received an urgent call there to see one of the AMOs, who had high blood pressure and had taken a bad turn. They did not realise that the new doctor had arrived, or they would have sent for him. This incoming week will be my last on the two practices.

The case of smallpox, which I mentioned in my last letter, died on the fifteenth day of illness with hypostatic pneumonia. After the first week of illness, when in a confused state, the patient decided to get his bow and arrow and go hunting for birds, and was out of isolation for three to four hours. His particular class are very keen on hunting, and they make very effective bows and arrows from springy bamboo. They fix a metal spear point to the arrow, and are occasionally able to shoot even a leopard. They are particularly keen on the wild fowl in the jungle. Fortunately, no one was infected, and the isolation system seems to have been satisfactory, as there have been no new cases. The whole labour force of the garden (about 2,000) was vaccinated, after receiving an urgent supply of lymph from Shillong.

The weather remains very hot and dry, and they say the water in the rivers is beginning to rise, but I haven't so far noticed much difference. The next dollop of rain should cool things a bit, and still the dust. We will probably lose the wooden bridge (over the Boroi River) in a month or so.

I attended someone about three weeks ago. He had been mauled by a bear, while hunting in the jungle. The bear, fortunately, had come up from the rear, and although the man's ribs were slightly exposed at some parts with the blows of the bear, no vital damage was done, and he has recovered very quickly.

We lost one of our bearers (personal servant) a week ago. He was a young fellow and very good. However, he decided to fall in love with another man's wife, and as the other chap was understandably not very pleased (and a bit heftier than the bearer), the pair decided to elope. I have heard nothing of them since. Reita decided to promote one of the "pani wallahs" (washing up boys), and he is certainly putting on a good show. We got servants' clothes from Calcutta, as is customary, and are now wondering how to get the new bearer squeezed into the set of the previous bearer, who was a very small chap...

Time is flying past very quickly. I feel I have very few spare minutes. We are becoming quite settled now, but get homesick occasionally. We have no difficulty in making ourselves understood now with the servants, and by the time we have been here a year, we should have a fair grasp of the language.

I had my first case of a snake bite in the district, a few days ago. The patient, who was working among the tea, suddenly appeared at the hospital in the manager's car. I quickly applied a tourniquet above the site to prevent absorption of poison, and gave the antivenom serum intravenously. The tourniquet can only be left on for half an hour, and as the patient was still free of symptoms at that time, I can only presume that it was a non-poisonous snake. The recent heat has been bringing them out of hibernation. Since the teeth marks were about half an inch to three-quarters of an inch apart, it must have been quite a big snake.

Tonight is the night for the Hindi film in the tea garden, and the servants were very keen to get finished quickly. The film is shown in the open air. All the tea gardens own a projector between them, and show a film to the labour force about once a month. Our club (Halem) borrows the machine, so we also get films about once a month. Some of the films are in English, as Hindi ones are not always available. When this happens, we pop over to see them. The last one was "King Kong", and it was as old as the hills! This evening, the "chowkidar" (night watchman) did not want to go, and got the job of bringing in our after-dinner tea at 9pm. We are getting used to him during the night. To begin with, we found it difficult to sleep owing to the sound of his snoring as he guarded our bungalow...

Dufflaghur Tea Estate, 4th May 1952

We are really very isolated out here. Despite the fact I have nearly 26,000 on the list, the European population is only two-dozen or less. I am hoping to find time to do all the interesting things I want to do, including further reading. I am still toying with the idea of taking an extra diploma or two, but until recently my time has been fully occupied.

I stopped attending the two districts fully two weeks ago. The new doctor (Arthur Chesshire) has got settled into his bungalow, and appears to be doing quite well. He seems a very nice fellow, and says he is going to "clean up the practice". I was telling him he would have to begin with soap and water...

Just now I am among the annual reports, which should have been written ages ago, but with my limited appreciation of local conditions, it was as well to wait. In any case, I was far too busy with two practices.

The river (Boroi) between the two parts of my practice is still manageable. The bridge, which has felt the strain following the recent thunderstorms, is tottering, and in a few weeks will be washed away. It is made entirely of bamboo, yet it can still take buses and lorries. It must be about seventy yards in length, and they continuously have to reinforce the bamboo supports. Once the bridge goes, I will have to cross by ferry boat, and owing to the trouble involved with that, I will not be taking too many unnecessary journeys.

The ferry on the River Boroi

When I first saw the ferry, I thought it could not possibly take a car over, but it does, even two at a time – one of them often being a bus or lorry. It is comprised of two very deep wide canoes with a platform between them, and is propelled by large poles. It will be November before a new (temporary) bridge can again be built.

Ferry carrying a bus

Lorry leaving the ferry

Passengers on the ferry

I was called in to see a man, following an accident in the factory yesterday.

The factory

There is a large master driving rod in all the factories, with varying sizes of driving wheels, at regular intervals, to accommodate belts which divide the various pieces of machinery. The engines vary between 100 and 150 HP in the various factories.

This man had been handling a belt which was hanging over the driving rod next to the wheel. It was not driving as it was disconnected from the sugar cane crushing machine. He had fallen in some way and tightened the belt, which immediately took grip of the driving rod, and carried him up to a height of about ten feet. He then managed to get his arm round the driving rod, and was rotated round with it until his arm parted company with him, and he fell to the floor, leaving his arm on the machinery.

The arm had been fractured in its middle third, and the muscles torn off, leaving about three inches of exposed bone. The brachial artery had been stripped, and owing to its elasticity had curled and made the control of haemorrhage easy.

I took the temporary dressing off this morning, and redressed it. Owing to gas gangrene infection, I have made no endeavour as yet to attend to bone or close the wound. I have put him on a huge dose of Penicillin, which should kill the gas gangrene, after which, we will be able to attend to the stump. The artery looked very precarious in any case, and even a small haemorrhage would have weighed the balance. I will let you know next time how he is getting on.

The manager on our tea garden at Dufflaghur is Mr Pattullo. He and his wife both come from Kirriemuir in Angus. On Sunday, I removed all his remaining teeth (eight in total). He had two concealed roots from previous "would be" extractions, and I was delighted to be able to get everything out, clean.

Mrs Pattullo comes over almost every evening, and has been very helpful to Reita settling in. Reita has become a great card fiend. Although she previously hardly knew one card from another, she has become quite an expert.

Left to right: Ina and Pat Patullo and Mum

My cars (Land Rover and Austin A70) are running quite well at the moment. I have a driver to attend to the details, and he is very good. He takes away my personal interest in the cars. Every other week, however, I inspect them on the ramp to see that everything looks adequately serviced.

I have taken a few more photographs, and will let you have copies quite soon. Meantime, I have enclosed a copy of our staff. They are, from left to right…

1. First bearer: the one that fell in love with another fellow's wife, and ran off with her, disappearing, since the former husband was a big tough fellow, and the couple were afraid. 2. Pani Wallah: the one that replaced the first bearer, but is now the second bearer in the dining room. As the Pani Wallah, he did the washing up. He is doing quite well in his new job. 3. Sweeper: he does all the floors in the bungalow, washing and odd jobs. 4. Cook's Pani Wallah: he used to do the washing up in the cookhouse, which is a separate building from the bungalow, and where all the cooking is done in very primitive conditions. He would carry the water (pani) from the well. The water is brown, and is boiled and kept in the fridge. He has now been promoted to "bottle washer khana Pani Wallah" and assists the second bearer at dinner. 5. Temporary driver, when my own one was away. 6. Cook. 7. Original second bearer: he is now the first bearer, and attends to the bedroom, clothes, etc. 8. Sitting down are the two maalis (gardeners). The night-watchman (chowkidar) is not there. He is the one that keeps us awake at night with his snoring. He will be away ploughing his rice land. Most of the servants are Hindus, but the cook is a Buddhist.

Mum

For about six months of the year, we were totally isolated because the temporary bridge was washed away. Allan went backwards and forwards with his work, but during that time, the only people I would see were the Pattullos and the servants.

Dufflaghur Tea Estate, 9th May 1952

Reita has fourteen hens now. She is getting quite expert at looking after them. Her job is to see that the servants do the feeding, watering, etc, and that they do not run away with too many eggs. They won't have much chance, as seven of the fowl are half-grown chickens, and three of the remainder are cocks, which will be going into the pot. A full-sized cock costs Rs 5 (7/6), and tastes very nice.

Until recently, the cook was "doing" us, left, right and centre. For a fowl, which is obtained in the bazaar, he would charge us Rs 6, instead of Rs 4 (medium sized), and was putting on so much, that I got one of the AMOs to buy for me. The cook, quite blatantly, took tomatoes, papaya and other vegetables from our vegetable garden and charged us for them in his weekly slip. We are gradually learning all the tricks.

I had a cat to attend to yesterday. It was only three-quarters grown, but was delivering kittens. After three days in labour, it had delivered a breech to the head, but the head had got stuck, and someone had managed to drag it out. The next kitten, a vertex presentation (head first), was completely stuck. It had a huge head, and I had a good laugh to myself as I delivered it with ovum forceps (normally used for removing aborted material), which fitted the head very well. On palpation of the abdomen, I could feel another kitten (a breech). She will manage to deliver this one as far as the head, and then someone can pull it out like the first one.

Mum

I don't remember Allan delivering these kittens, but I do remember he neutered a tom on another occasion. The cat belonged to the manager of Halem Tea Garden and his wife – Guy and Peggy Heefke. Unfortunately, the cat died under the anaesthetic, which was too strong. Peggy was understandably upset, and when Guy backed his vehicle out and killed the dog on the same day, Peggy came to the club dressed in mourning.

Dufflaghur Tea Estate, 6th June 1952

Our back garden is now empty. All the winter vegetables are finished, and the tropical stuff is not ready. We have two small banana trees, which will take a couple of years to grow, and a patch of pineapples, which will not be ready until nearer the end of the hot season. I have plans to get more banana tree cuttings planted. The oranges out here are like tangerines, but I will find out the procedure and get some planted. Grapes grow well, and also a fruit tree called a "litchi". I don't know what this tree is like, but the fruit is lovely. It is half-grape and half-plum and really delicious. We have kept the large central stones of some that were given to us, and will try to get seedlings — perhaps...perhaps...perhaps...

We had stewed mangoes as a dessert today, and these turned out to be very nice. Reita takes a walk round the back garden to see that the gardeners are keeping everything tidy. Since the "cook episode", she has been watching the vegetables!

Foot and mouth disease seems to be endemic in India. They take it for granted that there will be an outbreak every few years. Here, however, the death rate seems to be small.

The cows could hardly give less milk than they do at present, and it is quite a common thing to see a dead cow by the roadside being consumed by vultures. These fellows are like big turkeys, and go red in the face as they gobble over a large piece of flesh. Their resistance to disease must be exceedingly high. On the wing, they are slow, clumsy birds.

We have quite a few hawks, bigger than the ones at home, and almost identical in shape. I think I saw a large flock of swifts, last week. They were like swallows, but much smaller than the ones at home. There were none here all winter, and I was presuming they were coming from the south of India to nest here or in the foothills. There are other brightly coloured birds to be seen now and then. We last saw monkeys at the jungle picnic place more than a month ago, when they threw things from the trees at our Land Rover.

One of the workers was slightly mauled by a leopard on the tea garden last week, not two hundred yards from our bungalow. It had fallen asleep after some night prowling, and was disturbed by the tea pluckers. It has not reappeared since, and has probably changed its "digs"! We are getting used to this sort of thing. The only beast that is really feared is the bear, as it always makes a mess of anyone it mauls. Some of the frogs (hundreds of them) are very big and make a terrific noise at night, croaking in chorus. The mosquitoes are on the prowl, but have not reached their worst yet.

The fans over the bed are now on all night, and we have only a sheet. Despite the heat, I feel very energetic, and Reita has acclimatised well too. She has orchids and gardenias in the back garden now. They are in flower, and Mrs Pattullo is going to give her half a dozen eggs to put under one of the broody hens. These eggs are half Road Island Red and half local brew. The former breed does not do very well with the heat, and the latter has very small eggs – almost bantam style. It is only among the hills (Shillong, etc) that English breeds of hen, cow and sheep do well. The last batch of half-grown chickens worked out at five pullets and two cockerels. We were "done" by this arrangement, as the cock out here is more valuable for fighting purposes – and a bull in India is much dearer than a cow because of its value as a beast of burden.

I was out during Friday night at a tea garden ten miles away, attending to a labour case (the wife of one of the Indian staff). She was suffering from obstructed labour – her eighth baby. I stayed for three-quarters of an hour, but did not do anything as she was not ready. However, I got the head turned, and the baby delivered by forceps at midday yesterday, after the manager came for me by car. He told me they were in a terrible state of emotional unrest, and could not be consoled. I have seen her since, and the mother and baby daughter are doing very well. The number of obstructed labours out here is much less in proportion to population at home, as the babies are almost all premature and very small.

I see something out of the usual almost every other day. The tea garden I attended on Friday is the biggest in my district, and plans are going ahead for the construction of a maternity unit there. The plans have all been made to suit my suggestions, and it will give me great satisfaction to get this into proper working order after it has been built. This should be done next cold weather.

The price of tea in Calcutta is at crisis level just now, and all the managers are complaining bitterly. Competition from other parts of the world is getting very keen, and some of the recent prices have not been sufficient to clear expenses. This is not a very happy state of affairs, and the price of tea at home is going up. Where is the money going to between production and consumption?

The doctors at home seem to be getting a better deal now. The question of the "young doctor" seems to have been given some consideration, and the surgeries will now probably be at half strength. I always seem to miss the good bits of news like this on the wireless, but will get the low-down when you send the newspapers.

I sent the fellow who had his arm torn off in the factory to the Jorhat Mission Hospital, as his condition was poor. I have not heard how he is getting on, but he should be all right. I have had two other liver abscesses in the last two weeks – both men, and not very old. One died two hours after admission to hospital, and I did not see him until after death. The other was lying in hospital for five days (of which I was unaware) before I saw him during my routine visit. I operated under local anaesthesia and inserted a drainage tube. About one and a half pints of pus were removed. Unfortunately, his condition had deteriorated too far, and he died the same evening. I am past being annoyed at this sort of thing.

Mum

The hospital on Dufflaghur was just a dirty hut, and Allan kept fighting for improvements. The tea garden he refers to, where he wanted to build a maternity unit, would be Behali Tea Estate. The manager was English, and we knew him as "Brownie". His wife, Madge, was also English. As for those frogs – they were like an orchestra warming up. They were in amongst the rice, and we could hear them when we were in our beds.

Dufflaghur Tea Estate, 27th June 1952

We are both in the best of health and feeling energetic despite the heat. Our highest temperature to-date has been only 96 F, but the humidity has been as high as 90%. This means that the air has absorbed 90% of its possible uptake of water vapour, and has only 10% left in which to absorb sweat. The evaporation of sweat, which is nature's way of cooling the body, is therefore slowed.

Calcutta has had temperatures over 100 F, but the humidity is not usually quite so high. When we remember that the body temperature is somewhere between 97 F and 98.4 F, we realise that instead of having to keep its temperature above its surroundings, the body has to start keeping it below the surroundings when the temperatures are high. The animals with high normal body temperatures have therefore a decided advantage. The hens usually are quite unperturbed, but Reita says that her ones have drooping wings and sighing respiration at the moment.

Our fans are going all the time, and without them, one becomes fatigued in an enclosed space. I was amused to see how the manager's dog always lies on the hearth, where a cool draught is created by the chimney.

On Friday night we had thunder and lightning, during the course of which, a flash of lightning came so near, that it booted the voltage in the overhead electricity wires, and blew one bulb and the fuses in the bungalow. When we have storms, it can be pouring with rain where we are, and perfectly dry two miles away. Every night there is always lightning to be seen somewhere in the distance. We ended up with three inches of rain. Every stream in the district was full, and the roads were covered in water. It did not take long to clear, however, and since then, it has been absolutely dry with very strong sunshine.

The insects are now out in full force, but we take our Paludrine regularly, and should not have any trouble with malaria. There is a lot of malaria in the hospitals just now. The sickness rates are very high on all the tea gardens. Respiratory infections (coryza, bronchitis, influenza, pneumonia, etc) form the bulk of it at the moment. A near second, are bowel infections (diarrhoea, enteritis, dysenteries, etc). These latter are an indication of standards of sanitation. I have had a few sporadic cases of paratyphoid, but none of the full-blown thing.

There were no more cases of smallpox, and the climate is now not very suitable for spread of the disease. However, I see in the Calcutta newspaper that there has been a disastrous outbreak among the hill-tribes of the Naga Hills. They will be pleased to see the monsoon. It shows the value of regular vaccination.

I have a patient at the moment with a liver abscess. I have already drained two pockets of pus from her liver, but feel that she has another abscess forming in a different part of her liver. She came in at first with a severe pneumonia, then developed one abscess, which I drained between the ribs. The liver continued to enlarge, and I drained a further one with an upper abdominal incision, two weeks ago. She improved greatly after that, but her liver has started to enlarge again, and her heart is beginning to fail. Her general condition was so poor yesterday when I saw her, that I decided to do nothing. She will probably die, as she cannot possibly stand much more of this sort of thing. There has been so much pus that I doubt there is much healthy liver tissue left. A portable X-ray would be just the thing for letting me know where and how many abscesses are present. I will let you know what happens.

There was a case of rabies at one of the hospitals, a few weeks ago. The patient died shortly after admission, however, before I had time to see him. I have not yet seen a case of rabies.

We get the occasional case of tetanus – very often in new-born infants. It is the custom with some of the classes to dress the navel with cow dung, and what could be asking for it more? These cases almost always die, but in adults, the outlook is usually quite good.

We get a few cases of eclampsia. I was called to see a case, three weeks ago. The patient had been having convulsions, and was in a coma all day in her house before medical aid was sought. She was ready for instruments when I saw her, and after being put under with chloroform, I applied the forceps and started gentle traction. I was able to do absolutely nothing. When I measured the outlet of her bony pelvis, the shortest measurement was two and a half inches. Almost all of the infants are premature (anything from 2½lbs to 5lbs), so usually little difficulty is encountered. In this case, it was just too much. I had eventually to perforate the head of the infant in order to deliver her and stop her having fits.

Since this incident, we have been getting the mothers to come into hospital to have their babies under proper supervision. They are too fond of getting some old woman in to deliver their babies, and this affects the stillbirth and maternal mortality rates that are prevailing. By next cold weather, I now hope to have three maternity hospitals up and running, and have every normal case supervised by the trained midwife. These midwives are usually given a year's course of instruction at one of the mission hospitals, after which, they get a diploma. Given a proper chance, their results are really very good, and you can always be sure of a timely warning from them if anything goes wrong.

4

JULY TO SEPTEMBER 1952

Dufflaghur Tea Estate, 13th July 1952

It has been very wet for the last week, and some of the roads are flooded. All week, the sun has never been able to get through in full force, so it has been pleasantly cool.

We had dinner last night with Mr and Mrs Pattullo and a travelling Church of England padre, who will give a service tonight at the club. He was very interesting, and had been to Russia during the war. We have a service every few months, and occasionally it is a Scottish minister. The last Scottish minister and his wife (John and Anne Nelson) come from Stranraer. After tonight's service, we are attending the marriage of the daughter of the compounder (the man who dispenses medicines) from the Halem Tea Estate. The celebration will carry on for about a week, and will cost anything from Rs 1,000 to Rs 4,000 for a dowry. Quite often the bride and groom meet for the first time. If they do not like the look of one another, then it is too late!

Mum

I remember the wedding celebrations. There was lovely Indian food – curries and all the trappings. No alcohol, of course. They were Hindus.

It was a jolly time, and the celebrations would go on for days. But Allan and I just went to one function.

The padre Allan refers to was Padre Wylde. He was a lovely old man, and it was interesting listening to his stories.

Padre Wylde at a different function: third on left
Mum is in the middle wearing a hat

Dufflaghur Tea Estate, 23rd July 1952

I seem to have been kept on the hop since I started this letter. I do not know whether the newspapers will have had anything in them about floods and earthquakes. There was a tremor at Tezpur about a week ago, but of no severity. Some parts of Assam have had very damaging floods. Our rivers were certainly very wild, but too near the hills to have much chance of changing course, as they do in other parts.

The mails have been held up considerably, and we have not had your papers for a fortnight. No doubt they will all arrive in a bunch. I have arranged with Halem Tea Estate to send 2lbs of tea every month to you, in single containers. The 3lbs box requires a special licence, which has now been suspended.

Dufflaghur Tea Estate, 10th August 1952

One of the doctors in the neighbouring practice went home about three weeks ago. He had suffered from duodenal ulcers for years, and was fed up with it to such an extent that he arranged for the removal of the acid bearing part of his stomach (partial gastrectomy), in a London nursing home. We were absolutely amazed when we heard that he had died after the operation. He would be under forty years, and intended being such a short time at home that he decided to leave his wife with the children in Shillong. Life can be very hard.

Mum

I don't remember the doctor who died. Very sad, nonetheless.

Dufflaghur Tea Estate, 4th August 1952

It is almost impossible to believe it is now August. The seasons are so different. We have had quite a bit of heat, but not so much regular rain. The managers are complaining that it is not coming regularly enough. We get a terrific downpour, and then that really hot sun comes out again. We are faring quite well, nevertheless, and are beginning to discuss our two-week local leave. We will probably go up to Shillong (in the hills), but just cannot seem to work up a great deal of enthusiasm.

We can take the car over the Brahmaputra by river steamer, and motor up the hillside. The river has been giving quite a bit of trouble since the earthquakes, and has constantly been changing course – even more than usual. It is now about two or three miles wide, with sandbags at regular intervals, and so shallow in parts with the constant deposit of silt that the steamers get grounded every now and then.

The Company provides a holiday allowance, and there is some talk of this being substantially increased. All the tea garden staff have had a complete revision of their terms of service, with additions to the Provident Fund. I am waiting patiently to see if this will affect the medical officers. The reason for the rearrangement of salaries is because the price of tea has dropped so much this year, and the amount of commission received will fall very considerably. The terrific prices for tea seem to have gone forever. Just as with everything else, the seller's market has gone.

The wife of one of the managers was visiting her sister in Dooars, when the terrific floods hit that part of Assam. Some parts had nine inches of rain, and whole tea gardens were washed away, as well as the railway. They were isolated, unless by air. To get home, she had to fly right down to Calcutta and back up again to our district.

I had to do an amputation (mid-thigh) yesterday, for sarcoma. Reita came down to hand out instruments, while one of the AMOs (Dr Babu) and I amputated the limb.

Dad on his way to do the amputation
Austin A70 is behind him

Mum on her way to help Dad

It was fortunate that it occurred on a tea garden where the medical staff are young and helpful. Dr Babu, although very junior in service, is the most mentally active that I have in the district. The whole thing went like clockwork, with spinal anaesthesia – although during the operation, one of the ligatures slipped, and we had to take very quick and energetic measures to prevent bleeding. When I saw the patient today, she was satisfactory. The bone marrow, however, above the amputation site, was invaded by malignant growth, so the outlook is hopeless in any case. I wanted her to have the operation six weeks ago, but she and her family could not be convinced that it was so serious.

Mum

There were quite a few amputations, and Allan always took me to ensure cleanliness and sterilisation of equipment.

Dufflaghur Tea Estate, 23rd August 1952

This week has been very disturbing for Reita and the servants. The cook was stealing, and the more he got away with it, the more he became insolent. I finally had to relieve him of his duties. He is returning to Pakistan tomorrow.

Reita is "stewed" in the cookhouse, and working under primitive conditions (big black stove with coal and logs – and no gas or electricity) until we get another cook. The freshness of the food has improved considerably. We were blaming the goat for our poor meat, but it must have been the filthy fat the cook was using. Cooks are not available locally. Most of them come from around Chittagong in Pakistan.

The mails in Assam have been very upset since the flooding, and I hope you are getting our letters.

At the moment, I am reading the latest on malaria prophylaxis, so I can give the Company a considered answer to a recent letter. There is no doubt that Paludrine has not been the success that was initially promised, and the recent new anti-malarial drugs are more expensive (Chloroquine, Camoquin, Daraprim, etc). I have been wading through pages and pages of this stuff to get the most accurate, present-day opinion.

We went to see a film at the Halem Club last night, and owing to the heavy rain, had to plough through quite a bit of water to get there. At one point, it came right up to the floorboards of the Land Rover, but we were fortunate in getting through. The Newsreel gave us the Queen's birthday celebrations. This appeals to the Briton who is lost in another land!

Our back garden is not in very good shape just now. Our pineapples are about the only asset, and they are a late variety, so will not be ready until next month. As we chopped the top off each for eating, we put it back in the ground, and all have taken root. Our banana trees are very poor owing to the high Water Table at this time, and will not grow in the cold weather. The proper ground for them would be the front lawn, which is higher, but this raises complications.

A leopard was caught in a trap in one of the neighbouring tea gardens, and the manager has hung up the skin for us. The weather, however, might cause it to deteriorate before it is ready to go for curing. At the moment, it is drying with salt and alum.

Another manager shot a tiger (not too plentiful) with a single ball, twelve bore cartridge, but it managed to limp away into the jungle. They often become man-eaters when they are not able to catch up with wild animals following an injury. This one had killed about twelve buffalo, and the manager waited for it to come back, in a tree near its last kill. After the wounding, he was afraid it might cause damage, and drove a herd of buffalo into the jungle where it had disappeared. They did not scramble back in fright, so that part was searched, but nothing was found. The following day, the vultures were hovering around, and a stink was pervading a part of the jungle. They soon found the body with the ball right through its neck.

I have had one or two wee tiffs with some of the managers. They can be very exasperating. Each has his own wee area where his say is law, and sometimes they like to extend their orders to the visiting medical officer. Still, there is talk of us getting a portable X-ray in this district.

Unfortunately, the wireless has packed in, and I will have to send it to Tezpur by steamer.

Mum

Some of the managers wanted the Company to spend money on their things alone, and weren't interested in improving the medical service – so that could be a problem.

Still, we enjoyed the films very much. I think the film Allan is referring to is "Whisky Galore". I asked the Halem Club Committee (Holly, a tea planter, was the chairman) to get it. He also got "Coastal Command", which has scenes of Islay, and "The Maggie", which my father was supposed to be in as an extra. Unfortunately, he was edited out. However, there are many of the old folk I knew then in it. Fortunately, since it was an American film, my father still got his £5 a day!

Dufflaghur Tea Estate, 18th September 1952

Since the fall in the price of tea, I have been answering letters from Williamson Magor regarding proposed cuts in hospital developments. I no sooner get one lot cleared, when another lot arrives.

The last fortnight has been very wet, but we are always pleased to see the rain to bring down the temperature. Another month will see a marked change in the season. At the present moment, the roads are flooded with water, but this will clear quickly.

They have finished planting the rice (all by hand). By the time it has a month of heat and rain, it will have had a good start. When the fields go dry, it looks more like a crop of wheat than anything else.

I saw a very large cobra on the road today. A lorry was coming in the opposite direction, and when the driver saw it, he swerved the lorry and ran over it. He then stopped and backed over it again. Despite that, it managed to crawl away into the long grass. It was waving its head during this process, and I did not leave the car to investigate. It would have been about six to seven feet long. There are not very many of these fellows going about here.

We have been living very quietly. Reita is still cooking away, but we have arranged for a new cook to come tomorrow. I hope the quality of the food will be maintained. This fellow is a brother of one of the other cooks in the district, newly down from Shillong.

In one of your letters, you said I was needing a haircut. My barber comes every four or five weeks and gives me the old faithful bowl effort. My Rolls razor strap has been difficult to keep in order in this climate, so I have made up my mind to grow a beard after coming back from Shillong (local leave). I will cut it off again when the heat starts. We have not fixed up our holidays yet, but I will write to Shillong, the agents and the neighbouring doctor, this weekend.

Mum

Yes – Allan was always being told to cut down on hospital development expenses, and it used to annoy him. As for the cooking, I remember being back in the cookhouse. I didn't know how to make curries, so I'd throw something together. There was no running water, and we cooked on a coal fire. The servants would help, but it was up to me to produce the meal. There were no pots and pans. I had to use something that was like a pot, but had no handles. The only vegetables we would have in September would be tinned. They would be sent up from Calcutta. We would only just be starting to plant the vegetables and flowers in the back garden. The heat in the cookhouse was terrible because the fire would be on all the time.

Dufflaghur Tea Estate, 19th September 1952

It is now more than a year since we left Falkirk, and it has been the shortest year I have known. We are in really good form and well acclimatised now. We take a small Paludrine tablet every day to keep the malaria parasites at bay.

I am pretty well versed in all the tropical conditions, and find that most of the illness is due to conditions that could quite easily occur at home. Unfortunately, I do not have Falkirk Royal Infirmary to help me out, as I used to have, and have to set all the fractures, etc, unless there are special complications, when I send them by river steamer to the Mission Hospital on the south bank of the Brahmaputra – the journey being up to sixteen hours away.

The AMOs are very helpful and handle all the routine coughs and colds, pneumonias, etc, without any difficulty. They have a licentiate degree, following a four-year course, which qualifies them for such work. The Calcutta MB, BS is equivalent to our own degree, and is recognised in the UK as such. Unfortunately, owing to the amount of British capital in Tea, there are not very many Indian doctors in the industry.

I managed to get one pound of tea dispatched to you from Halem Tea Estate, in August, and one to Willie (*Dad's brother*), early this month. I have received special permission for 3lbs, and will get one more dispatched, next month, as well as the one pound from Halem. The tea is not at its best just now, as the growth is too rapid, but it will be better in October.

The amputation case is doing very well, but the eventual outlook is very guarded.

There was an outbreak of rinderpest at Halem a few weeks ago. I had a good look at all the animals, and now have a good book on the pathology of the cow. I am really quite interested in this animal, and hope we will be able to have some within a few months. The only drawback is – who will do the milking?

Mum

I remember the discussion about getting a cow. My question was: "Who the hell's going to milk it?" I certainly wasn't. If Allan had had the time, he could have milked it, since he'd milked his father's cows as a boy. In any case, the Pattullos had cows, and I used to buy milk from them.

Mum with the Pattullos' cows

Dufflaghur Tea Estate, 30th September 1952

We have had a new cook for more than a week now, and he is very much better than the previous fellow. Reita has become a lady of leisure again – some hope! She keeps an eye on everything that is being done, and has now gone far beyond the corporal stage, and will qualify as sergeant major any day!

Our wireless is now back in commission. One of the resistances had burned out. I got a new one sent up from Tezpur, and one of the managers fixed it in for me. We are having a film show on Thursday at the club. We look forward to these very much when we are isolated so much now.

We had a tiger outside our window two nights ago – fierce, growling. All our windows were wide open and only covered with mosquito wire. We were quite pleased when he departed, and it did not take me long to fix the windows in an almost closed position. I might add that during the tiger's visit, our night watchman, who was on the veranda at the time, slept peacefully like a baby...

There has not been a great deal of animal life recently. Tigers very seldom go into the mud and bamboo houses, and the Indian is perfectly confident that they will not do this. Now and again, however, they run away with a cow or a dog, and it seems to be a well-known fact that the tiger is fond of a "doggy breakfast". The vulture is not the aggressive fellow that one is led to believe. He clears away all the decaying flesh. The hawk, however, is very aggressive, and runs away with all the chickens whenever he gets a chance. I was watching Reita feeding the hens on Sunday (we have seventeen now), and they all suddenly scattered under the hedge, following which, a big hawk came swooping over. I will have to get a .22 rifle some time!

The harvest celebrations have just finished. All the rice has been planted, and the rain will not be very heavy now. In a couple of weeks, it will be completely finished. The nights are quite cool, but we haven't stopped using the fan yet.

The Tea Industry is hoping for the finish of rationing. There is now a glut, and the prices do not always clear the cost of manufacture. Some of the tea gardens in Darjeeling have already closed down, as there is no demand for quality tea. The public only wants cups to the packet. Cuts in tea garden expenses are being made everywhere, and medical development plans are being temporarily abandoned.

Mum

Bloody gun, again! He never, ever mentioned it to me. Probably because he knew what I'd say! The hawks and vultures were all the same to me, with their dirty big wings. I remember hearing a story from a manager's wife. When she first came out to Assam, as an innocent young bride, her husband told her that the type of hawk in Assam was called a "shite hawk" – for obvious reasons. She hadn't heard this kind of language before, and one evening, she advised a table of dignitaries that the worst bird in Assam was the "shite hawk".

5

OCTOBER TO DECEMBER 1952

Dufflaghur Tea Estate, 1st October 1952

Reita has read an article in the paper confirming the end of tea rationing. We must have missed it on the wireless. I am surprised no one has mentioned it, since it has such an important bearing on the industry.

I wrote my agents a very long letter regarding malaria in the district, ten days ago. I covered absolutely every aspect of it. It took me a month to think about, collect statistics and write. However, they thanked me profusely for it.

We are thinking about going to Shillong in November, and will require heavy clothes at that time. It will be nice to appreciate a fortnight of British weather! Although it is cold at night here at the moment, the sun is strong during the day.

Our cook is going to Shillong for a week on Thursday to collect his wife and family. Reita will be back on the job again! I hope he does not take the notion not to return, as he is a good chap. We're always hungry now. We lost a bit of weight during the heat, but are beginning to put it on again.

I am still doing my rounds, as usual. The new doctor in the neighbouring practice (Arthur Chesshire) is away down to Calcutta to meet his wife, and I am hoping I do not get any urgent calls to his district, as it is time-consuming at the river crossings and on the bad roads. I also hope they manage to get the bridges built quickly, for although the rain will be finished quite soon, the water from the hills will remain until the end of November, or the beginning of December.

Mum

Yes – poor Reita was back in the cookhouse!

Dufflaghur Tea Estate, 22nd October 1952

The cook has returned, and is presenting us with appetising food.

The new cook

Our servants, however, keep us on our toes. On Monday, one of the bearers was on leave and the other one arrived to serve dinner in an inebriated condition. I had to give him medication to sober him up! A few days later, Reita discovered that her salt and pepper dishes were broken (two chickens with holes in the head). When she enquired as to the cause, it was carefully explained that the hens had come in, and being attracted to them, broke them. It is usually the cat that gets the blame – only we don't have one!

Last weekend was a public holiday – the equivalent of our Christmas and New Year. We went to see a show on Saturday evening. There were large marquees, and the managers had laid on temporary electricity. The set-up reminded me of our "shows" at home, with stalls for all sorts of nuts and sweets. There were two main shows. The one we saw was performed by the factory boys. Women are not allowed to take part, but some of the men dressed up as women, and they all gave us a great display of love and war dances with the drums booming out at a terrific rate. It was almost like something you would see at the pictures. Eventually, a man dressed up as a woman with a pregnant abdomen and a terrific head of hair, came out and started having a row with "her" husband. It ended with a kick on the protuberant abdomen, much to the delight of the onlookers...

We have had an exceptional amount of rain in the first half of this month, but the heavy rain is now more or less finished. The river, which I cross on Mondays and Tuesdays, is now much better, and will not give me too much bother. The temporary bridge (bamboo) over the Boroi, will be completed by the end of November. Plans for a permanent bridge have been passed by the Central Government at the cost of Rupees 16 laks (£120,000). Work is starting in the cold weather of 1953.

We have a small first batch of vegetables sown (turnips, carrots, etc), and some cabbages and cauliflowers planted out from boxes on the veranda.

The Water Table in the garden was up to two inches from the surface until recently. All the plants must be planted early in the morning, or in the evening, owing to the strong sun. Small shades have to be slanted over them. A banana tree gives suitable pieces of bark, which can be cut to suit. We hope to have some flowers planted by next week.

Mum on the veranda with the vegetables planted out in boxes

I have decided to postpone the beard until the weather is much cooler. My razor is now working all right, in any case.

We have made arrangements to go up to Shillong for the last week in November and the first week of December. Shillong is quite near, as distances go out here (about two-hundred and fifty to three-hundred miles away). We board the steamer at our own "ghat" (pier), which is seven miles from the tea garden, and cross the Brahmaputra during the night. We disembark on the south bank in the early hours of the morning, and after motoring for eighty to one hundred miles, come to the first gate. All traffic is one-way on the hill, and there are different times for going up and coming down. We will be able to let you know all about it from Shillong.

Mum

I remember the broken salt and pepper dishes. My sister, Cathy, had given them to me. It was a hen and a cock. I recall being told that the real hens must have jumped on the table to swipe them off! We didn't have children then, so they couldn't blame them. The servants would get drunk at times. They used to drink something called "Sulai pheni", which was a very strong home brew.

Dufflaghur Tea Estate, 4th November 1952

There is still no bridge between the two parts of my practice, and I have often been delayed with the ferry sticking in the shallow parts. The road to the jungle picnic place is being opened just now, and we will be able to have more exercise and swimming.

There is a rogue elephant on the far side of the tea garden just now. It is coming in and eating and trampling the growing rice crop. I went with two of the assistant managers, who are keen on shooting, to see if it could be spotted (at dusk). Unfortunately, it had already been out that morning, and having had a good feed, was back in the jungle. The villagers were very worried about the rice crop. The rifle used for this job is a 0.45-inch, or a 0.47-inch.

Reita's hens are now laying well. She has eight laying hens, and we are getting five to seven eggs daily. There are also the half-grown ones that will soon be laying as well. Our cook is settling in quite well, and giving us appetising food. Our tomatoes are now planted, but they will take a wee while to grow.

I have been doing quite a bit of medical reading in the last few months (Synopsis of Tropical Medicine by Sir Philip H Manson-Bahr).

A few days ago, Reita and I did another amputation operation for gangrene of foot. Things went off very well, and the patient (quite a young man, about forty years, with degenerative changes in the arteries of his right leg) is now doing fine. I took the leg off just above the knee. When I examined the popliteal artery (behind the knee) after the operation, it was thickened to such an extent, that only a fine point could get into the lumen (channel in the centre). We will get some sort of artificial limb made on the tea garden, and he will be fit as a night watchman. During the operation, a fly, which had managed to get into theatre, landed on my back, and the compounder, no doubt thinking about germs, gave me a clatter on the back to kill it. No thanks to him that I didn't start amputating the other limb! However, I was ready to close the wound by that time.

The girl who had amputation for sarcoma of leg, is now doing well, and her haemoglobin has come up. She had rather a sticky course. It is to be hoped that there are no more malignant seedlings in other parts of the body, but she will be most fortunate if there are not. She was riddled with malaria at the same time, but her spleen and liver are now normal. I had wondered, at the time, if the enlarged liver might be an early secondary.

We went to the first dance of the cold season (there are none during the hot weather) on Saturday at a neighbouring club (Bishnauth), and had a nice evening. It is now more than a year since we arrived in Assam, and the time has simply flown. We still think we will return home after completion of our first tour, but it is difficult to be certain.

Mum

There were a few rogue elephants. In fact, one of the managers took a photo of Allan and me in the river at the picnic spot (Boroi) when we were about to run away from another elephant. We didn't know the photograph was being taken.

Dad and Mum running away from an elephant!

I was involved in quite a few amputation cases. I remember the one Allan writes about. The compounder thumped Allan on the back when a fly landed on him. It was so hot, someone must have left a window open.

Dufflaghur Tea Estate, 17th November 1952

We are going up to Shillong on Sunday 23rd November, and will arrive there at 10am on the 24th. We will be leaving Shillong on Friday 5th or Saturday 6th December, and will be back on the tea garden by Sunday 7th December, at the latest. Our address in Shillong will be: c/o Pinewood Hotel, Shillong, Assam.

There are quite a few cases of malaria (relapses) just now with the sudden change in the weather. It has become chilly in the evening, and we are almost ready to light a fire. The cook had a temperature of 103 F last night; however, after some Chloroquine (new treatment), his temperature rapidly fell, although he still looks a bit seedy. He has been taking it very easy today. I developed a very nasty "cold" myself, about ten days ago, and succeeded in getting my sinuses clogged up. They are beginning to clear now, but I have developed a cough at night. Although full of complaints (Reita says), I have not been fevered or off work, but most of the European staff have been down with "flu". I have a lot of letters that keep coming in, and were piling up while I had the "cold". I am determined to get my letters written tonight. I do not hear so many complaints now from the managers regarding tea prices. The London market seems to have improved quite a bit; nevertheless, the agents are pressing them all very hard now to keep down expenses, and all development schemes have been abandoned.

Mum

No doubt I was back in the cookhouse when the cook was ill. Fortunately, I don't remember this incident. The cook was really good. You only had to show him a picture of something, and he could replicate it. His puddings and cakes were lovely.

Dufflaghur Tea Estate, 10th December 1952

We had some fun getting to Shillong. At the first river crossing, sixteen miles from here, we got stuck in the sand for a short time, before getting on to the ferryboat. The water is so low just now, that three-quarters of what was river, is now sand.

At the next crossing (sixty miles from here), we developed a petrol leak from the pipe leading from the tank at the back, but the driver stuck it up with soap before we lost too much petrol. When we arrived at Tezpur, the ferry (a large motor one) was late. By the time we got on, and went round a new long sandbank in the Brahmaputra, and arrived at Silghat on the opposite bank, it was 6pm (three hours later), and we had left home at 7am.

We then had over one hundred miles to motor to the first gate. We reached it about 9.30pm, only to discover we were too late to go up the hill. We drove on a further twelve miles to Gauhati (Guwahati) to look for accommodation, but the only suitable places were full up. So, after trailing round the town, we went back to the gate and slept in the car until 4am, when we were able to start the fifty-three-mile ascent.

We arrived at the hotel about 6.30am, almost twenty-four hours after we had left home, and the only food in that time was a few sandwiches. We had breakfast and went off to bed.

For the first two days of our stay, there was no sun owing to the clouds, and it was so cold that we were ready to go home. Our room had not been recently fired, and it took us those days to heat up. After that, we began to enjoy our stay at the hotel, which is five thousand feet up in the hills.

We had a run up to the top of the hills (six to seven thousand feet), where we took photographs. We met a young couple from Stirling (Neil and Sheila Campbell), who came out ten months ago. He is an assistant manager on a tea garden near Jorhat on the south bank (of the Brahmaputra). They have invited us to Jorhat, which means that I will be able to go to the Assam Branch of the next BMA meeting in Jorhat (probably March 1953) with Reita, and stay with them.

Dad and Mum in Shillong

Sheila and Neil Campbell in Shillong

The hotel was very hospitable. The food was lovely – four course breakfast, six course lunch and seven course dinner. You could eat as much as you wanted. We were not long in getting to know the various people. There was another doctor from one of the more hard-hit areas there, at the same time. He was saying he was having a terrific job trying to cut down medical expenses, and some of his tea gardens had been running at a loss for two to three years.

In other areas with special difficulties, the tea gardens are just closing down. Our area, however, appears to be quite good, since it is more isolated with plenty of "khat" land (paddy land) round about. The eventual cost of tea manufacture, per pound, is much less than in the areas near big towns, where the village populations are so much greater. The average cost of producing tea ranges from Rs 1/3 to Rs 1/9, or Rs 1/10. If you multiply the difference by the number of pounds produced, the amount is fantastic. When you consider that the various grades of tea are now selling (here and on the London market) about the equivalent of Rs 0/14 to Rs 1/7, or Rs 1/8, you can understand the headaches that are produced. The methods of plucking and manufacturing are being altered. Low grades of tea are being eliminated as much as possible, since they are quite sure to sell at a loss, and the overall average will be kept as near the highest grades as possible.

I am wondering how all this will affect me, but conditions will possibly show some improvement in a year or two. The mere fact of eliminating the less economical tea gardens (although hard) might help the other ones. They also say that this year's prices have been affected by the sudden release of hidden stocks of tea at home – end of rationing.

On the way home, on Saturday, we came down the hill after 7am, and were able to see the scenery (dark on the way up). At every corner there are drops of hundreds of feet (no barriers), and the road winds so sharply that one is not encouraged to put the foot very heavily on the gas. Fine trees grow everywhere, but at least there is a tar surface to give you reasonable control of the vehicle.

Halfway down the hill, our hydraulic brakes got jammed at the front, and the driver had to bleed some of the brake fluid to release them. After that, we succeeded in getting down the hill just before the line of traffic was due to change direction. We decided to go home by a different route, and motored to Gauhati (Guwahati), twelve miles from the bottom gate, where the Brahmaputra is narrow. We got over on a ferry (a good bit bigger than the Queens Ferry one), and it only took twenty minutes.

We had only completed about twenty miles of the one hundred and eighty-five mile run up the north bank of the Brahmaputra, when the petrol pipe, which had been welded in Shillong, snapped, and we had an awful job joining it with a piece of hosepipe, ten times too wide. It took us three hours to reach a small town, twenty miles further on, during the course of which, the hosepipe kept jumping off. It was lucky we had a spare tin of petrol (four gallons), which we put in the tank in small quantities to prevent total loss. A wee fellow in the small town (Mangaldai) took the petrol pipe between his toes, and gave us a weld that one would expect in the best garage in Glasgow. I gave him Rs 6, and he was delighted.

Despite all our mishaps on the way back from Shillong, we enjoyed the run, and had taken the precaution of arming ourselves well with sandwiches, boiled eggs, boiled potatoes in the skin, orange juice, etc, before we left the hotel.

Since I came back on Monday, I have been on the trot all the time: two liver abscesses, gallstones, etc. They had been cooking for quite a few days, awaiting my arrival, since the AMOs are reluctant to bring the neighbouring doctor on a run of thirty or forty miles.

Mum

Funnily enough, the couple we met from Stirling also took photographs of Allan and me, and when they showed them to their friends in Scotland, one of them turned out to be my cousin, Bessie Allan. The Pinewood Hotel in Shillong was lovely – apart from the arum lilies. I didn't like them because they're for funerals.

Dufflaghur Tea Estate, 21st December 1952

I have not gone out to work this morning. I have decided to catch up with all the clerical work that has accumulated. Reita is away to the

Halem Club to do a wee bit in preparation for a Christmas party. The children in the district (and the neighbouring one) are all coming to it. No energy has been spared to make this a success. So far as I understand, all the adults will be in attendance as well to watch the antics of Santa, who is arriving by elephant to distribute presents. One of the young fellows in the district will be dressed as Santa, and we are all hoping he does not fall off the elephant's back!

Mum

I remember this very well. We prepared food, and sorted records to play on the gramophone. I'm pleased to say that Santa did not fall off the elephant.

6

JANUARY TO MARCH 1953

Dufflaghur Tea Estate, 11th January 1953

I have been making good use of the book on tropical medicine (*Synopsis of Tropical Medicine*). I am getting very interested in malnutrition and all the deficiency states. My biggest headache at the moment is trying to reduce the drug bill without upsetting treatment. I need to cut out the delicacies of treatment, the value of which is doubtful or temporary, and I have spent weeks on this.

The doctor from the practice near Tezpur (eighty odd miles from here), who is at present on home leave, has sent word that he will not be back. I do not know what they will do about this vacancy, as at present it is being occupied temporarily by an old retired fellow.

A fortnight or so ago, two brothers from the labour force decided to have a row after getting drunk. One fellow made fifteen lacerations on the other with a pruning knife. When I saw him, the AMO had already inserted fifty stitches to various parts of his body, but mainly the head and face. He could not, however, cope with the left wrist and forearm, which were almost severed in two, and had to have a tourniquet on continuously. We amputated the arm above the elbow that evening, without any hitches, and he is doing very well.

Mum

Allan had his hands full. I remember him almost tearing his hair out trying to organise the drugs. As for "Sulai pheni", it was a terrible drink. It made them go mad and do really stupid things.

The old doctor was a Colonel Logan. He'd actually retired, but came back. He'd worked on Dufflaghur at one time, and during the war was a colonel in the army. I believe he was the one who showed the bearers how to do their work in an efficient and organised manner.

Dufflaghur Tea Estate, 21st January 1953

We have not seen any wild animals for a long time now, but the neighbouring tea garden lost two cows, during the day, about three weeks ago. It must have been a hungry tiger, for a leopard seldom comes out to hunt during the day. It would appear the herdsmen were taking all the cows to new pastures, and two wandered into the jungle. Since the cows are very small, a tiger can carry one away without any bother.

The scarcity of grass is always very acute during the cold weather, and the cows gradually become skin and bone. There is no question of winter-feeding, as this would deprive the people. The reason for grass scarcity is the lack of rain with the relatively strong sun, which burns everything up. If some of the rainfall could be spread over the cold season, this would be one of the most productive areas in the world.

The rate of growth of vegetables (cabbages, cauliflowers, turnips, etc), which are watered by the gardeners, is really terrific. The only difficulty is the presence of various fly larvae in the soil, which have a chew at the tomatoes, etc. It is often necessary to spray the ground with DDT solution.

We have been eating cauliflowers for about three weeks now, and they did not go into the soil until the latter half of October. Our flower seeds, however, are a flop. Only about one-third germinated, and they look pretty miserable (dahlias, cosmea, hollyhock, poppies, linaria and sweet peas). The agents send a tin of seeds every year.

Some of the other folks have been complaining of the poor germination, and it may well be the suppliers were getting rid of some old stock, and mixed it with the rest of the seeds! Nothing would surprise me more.

Three of our servants have been repatriated to Central India (completion of contract), and the tea gardens are trying to cut the labour forces this year. Unfortunately, I had to sack my driver at the beginning of the New Year. He was getting very lazy and would not look after the vehicle properly. The crowning blow was when he got drunk and bumped a bullock cart, bending the front mudguard in the process. We had a set-to, and he gave me so much cheek, I had no alternative.

My new fellow is doing quite well at the moment. He has a much more pleasant disposition, but has no licence yet. Nonetheless, he is very willing and level-headed. He does the work on the vehicles, while I read his instructions from the service manual. He was driving a lorry on the tea garden previously, but has been working with vehicles for the last eight or so years. He was born on Halem Tea Estate, and must be about thirty years old. Most of the workers do not know their exact ages.

Johan, the driver

He does my "on-garden" driving, and is well experienced. When he went for his test at the police station for his lorry licence this month, he was failed because he did not know the road signs, and no one had gone over them with him beforehand. He has to wait another six months before the inspector comes round again. In any case, you would have to go some distance up the bank of the Brahmaputra before seeing any of the road signs on the test charts. They are mostly different from the ones at home, and there are many more to cope with the almost complete illiteracy of the drivers in this part of the world.

The Land Rover was over at the car agents on the south bank for re-boring, etc. The bill came to Rs 1,500, but it is now running very well. I have nothing to do with vehicle bills, which is a good thing, since costs are about double those at home.

The Austin A70 has been giving a bit of trouble. The crown wheel screwing nuts sheared off a while ago, and churned up in the differential gear box. The agents have now arranged to send up a Morris Oxford, which Douglas Taylor brought out. He was one of the assistant managers we met on the ship over, and he and his wife are now in Africa. The car has been lying in a storeroom for a year, and has only done about five thousand miles.

The sickness rates in the hospitals are very low just now. This is the healthy part of the year. I am still doing the survey of medical costs to see if economies can be made. The bill for last year was Rs 60,000 to Rs 70,000 (roughly £5,000) for the district as a whole, and was even greater the previous year.

It is a big job pricing the medicines to see which are the luxuries and which are not. I am trying to find which preparations are the best buy, and the differences in the prices of similar products out here are really terrific. Luminal (phenobarbitone made by Bayer) costs Rs 16 per ounce. Gardenal (phenobarbitone made by M&B) costs Rs 4 per ounce. You can see the difficulties involved when you consider that these two preparations are equally effective in treatment.

Mum

The cows were sacred, so couldn't be killed. That's why they got so thin. They would hobble around, until they eventually died on their feet. The poppies were interesting. When we first came out, the Pattullos told us that a few years previously, no one had been allowed to grow them in case they were turned into opium.

Dufflaghur Tea Estate, 25th January 1953

We had quite an adventure at the weekend. Rain started on Friday, and by the time it had finished on Saturday morning, it had deposited one and three-quarter inches on us. This has not happened at this time of year for eight years. A couple, who are due to go on home leave in March, had arranged a party for Saturday evening at their bungalow (fourteen miles from here), which is even more isolated than ours. Unfortunately, the Public Ways Department had decided to improve a part of the road which was badly washed away during the monsoon. They had piled about one to one and a half feet of earth on the road for a distance of two hundred yards, with a view to having it packed down by the passing traffic, after which, they would resurface it with shingle. You can imagine what happened when the rain came. The place was a mass of soft slipping mud. We were fortunate in that we had been given early warning of it, and we decided to take the Land Rover by daylight. All the other cars had to park on one side of the bad part, whilst the visitors were conveyed to the party by tractor.

On the way home at 1am, we decided to hold back to make sure none of the visitors had any difficulties on any other part of the road. By the time we negotiated the bad part again (more rain had fallen), my wheels were slipping all over the place, and eventually landed in the ruts made by the lorries and buses, which were too deep to keep my differentials (back and front) off the mud. We stuck fast, and had to wait for daylight to get a squad to push us out. We were frozen and miserable when we arrived home, and have spent the day in bed.

I had a call to Halem Tea Garden in the early hours of Thursday morning. Two young fellows from the Halem workforce had been coming back from fishing (so they say), when they met a Punjabi and two others (all drunk) from the village. They exchanged some rude remarks, and when I saw one of the young fellows, he had a stab wound (from below, upwards) in the centre of his abdomen, and four feet of intestine prolapsing through the wound. I cleaned the grass and twigs off his intestine, and returned it to the abdomen, after repairing the perforation. He also had another stab wound below the heart, with a shattered rib and extensive internal bleeding. I tried to patch him up, but it was hopeless, and he died the next morning from exsanguinations. He and his brother had been up to no good during the night, and had got more than they bargained for.

This tea garden has had three or four murders in the last few years, mostly the result of drink which is illegally brewed in the villages. The police raid the producers every now and then, but a fine of Rs 1,000 means nothing to them.

I have never seen a bear, only the result of an attack. They are fickle creatures, and their aggressiveness is due to fear. The most feared of the animals, nevertheless, is the wild elephant that can turn a car over and trample it to bits. One of the tea planters was telling us that when he first came out, he had an old car that gave him a lot of problems starting. On one such occasion, he was returning from a shooting expedition, and was trying (with difficulty) to start the car, when an elephant came on to the jungle road and charged him. The elephant gave the car such a dunt at the back (it was in gear), that the car started, and went flying down the road to safety. He was afraid to tell his wife of the incident in case she stopped him going on shooting expeditions, and the first she heard of it was in the Calcutta office, about a year later – much to her surprise and dismay.

Mum

I remember the incident in the mud very well. On that occasion, I didn't get dirty, but there were plenty other times we got coated in mud. One such time was when we were with the acting manager on Dufflaghur (Jack Fea) and his wife, Elizabeth. The Pattullos were on leave. We were all dressed in evening attire, and returning from a party. The Land Rover, as usual, got stuck in the mud, and we all had to get out to push, whilst Allan steered. Suddenly the vehicle started, and moved forward, causing Jack to fall flat on his face in the mud. All we could do was laugh.

Jack Fea with a domesticated elephant at Mangaldai, Assam

Left to right: Elizabeth Fea and Xander Fea (son) with Mum

Dufflaghur Tea Estate, 8th February 1953

Despite all the talk of world upheaval, we are living very peacefully in Assam. I was, however, surprised one day when I looked at the map and discovered that we are so close to China, Tibet and Burma (Myanmar), but the natural obstacles are so great that I should imagine that we will not be much affected. During the war, it was a very bedraggled Japanese army that got through the hills from Burma, and by that time they were incapable of doing anything. The mountains along the borders are almost impassable for forces in numbers. I feel quite reassured that there are many safety valves available to blow off, before we might be affected.

The manager of the neighbouring garden saw an elephant crossing the river where we have our picnics. He was worried at first, in case it might be frightened and attack him, but it just lifted its trunk, snorted and went on its merry way. Everyone has a healthy respect for the wild elephant. It can catch a tiger with its trunk and crush it to the ground, but tears in its hide, made by tigers, are very liable to go septic and produce serious wounds. One of the great hunters in the district, who goes into the jungle frequently to hunt, tells the story of a bull elephant that charged his elephant. His got down on its knees, and took the impact straight on. There was a shudder, and the wild bull bounced back to the side with a broken neck. When you pass a domesticated elephant on the road, it usually turns to face you until your car passes.

Domesticated elephants on the road

The temperature has started to change again. We have been spending every Sunday at the picnic place. Within another three weeks, we will be able to stay in the water indefinitely, without feeling chilled. We have had no fire in the evening now for a few days, but will probably require it again for a short time, if there are some dull rainy days.

The wooden bridges (road) are being repaired for the 1953 monsoon. Recently, the Public Ways Department have put a scheme under way to divert a river into a different drainage area. This will bring a considerable amount of extra water under and over my outlet road. Last year, without the extra water, there were days when the water came right up to the level of one particular bridge, but did not go any further because it had already washed the road away on either side, and this formed a safety valve. This year, they have brought the road up a level, and with the extra water, this bridge is sure to go. I will have to try and find a way out through the other garden, which is relieved of the water.

I finally got the names of some of the shade trees: albizzia stipulata, albizzia procera and Pithecellobium saman. They have different ones to suit different stages of the tea tree. If the tea bush were not pruned, it would grow ten to twelve feet high, like an open hedge. As it is now, it covers the whole surface area at a flat level of about two or two and a half feet, with big permanent shade trees every twenty yards, or slightly less. The tea bush itself depends on bacterial breakdown of vegetable or animal matter for the supply of nitrogen, or in the form of sulphate of ammonia, which is the main fertiliser used. Sulphate of ammonia is so scarce in India that the Government regulates its supply.

Mum

I vaguely remember that at the time there was some kind of discord with China. I didn't know much about it, but my main concern was, if we had to run away, how would I manage to take all the linen I'd collected with me?!

Dufflaghur Tea Estate, 30th March 1953

We have had the most unusual weather this year. The roads are usually dry and very dusty at this time, but not this year. Can you imagine our plight? I have been careful in avoiding the possibility of getting stuck in the mud. I did not manage to get to the other end of my practice today, but got an urgent call to a more accessible part. The ruts on the road are anything up to a foot deep. However, one day of strong sun is like a magic wand to the mud.

The Calcutta folk have not been very lucky. Having no clouds or rain to keep things cool, the temperature shot up to 104 F one day. We have had no high temperatures yet, but are glad to have the fan ticking over. When the rain finishes, we will probably get it hard and sore. The tea planters are expecting a hot monsoon.

We have been going to the picnic place every week, but have not always been successful. One week it rained so hard that we were soaked to the skin. This did not prevent us from bathing in the middle of it all. Our journey to the jungle is something that keeps one week from slipping into the next.

Dad posing at the picnic place

Mum posing at the picnic place

Dad doing a handstand at the picnic place

Our films (once a fortnight now) also help. We are due one on Saturday if the mail bus manages to get through. We are almost halfway through our contract. The rumour goes that if you renew it, the remuneration is much increased, but I suppose that will depend to some extent, on the price of tea. They are cutting expenses left, right and centre in the industry, but the prices have recently shown some slight improvement. This part of Assam, which was most recently converted from jungle to tea, is not as badly hit as other parts, where the bushes are longer in the tooth, and the soil is less helpful.

I am glad your wallpapering and painting has been a good success. We do not have wallpaper out here. The dampness in the air would loosen it in two days. The mosquitoes are out in force once more, and anti-malarial measures are again active. We still dabble away with our Paludrine, and have very good health – touch wood!

Our vegetables in the back garden are now almost finished. We have had quite a good year, but don't spend enough time on it. My "maali" (gardener) told me it was time to get some "goon dhan" (Indian corn) planted to get it ripened before the monsoon (middle of June). Our pineapples are now showing some signs of life, but we will be sorry to lose our peas, cabbages, etc, as these are now finished, and pumpkins, etc, are a very poor substitute. With the rain just now, the grass is all growing, and the cows have not developed the starved appearance which is usual at this time when the grass gets burned up. I have been having a bit of trouble with my Land Rover recently, and the Morris is not fit to cope with the roads. The coil and battery have gone – "karab hogia" (bad!). However, I have sent for a good supply of spares to see me through the monsoon. I have had more experiences of cars than ever before, but I have been lucky in avoiding major mechanical catastrophes. I am collecting data and statistics for the various annual health reports at the moment. I hope to complete them within a month, this year. It was terrible last year. I had only been in the district for two months of 1951, and knew nothing of the local conditions. I completed the last one for 1951 in September 1952, and was told afterwards, that I was not really expected to do them for 1951!

7

APRIL TO JUNE 1953

Dufflaghur Tea Estate, 16th April 1953

We were very pleased to receive your letters, and surprised that you had not received a letter from Assam for five weeks. I wrote about two weeks ago, and am wondering if the old postmaster put the letter in with the ordinary mail by mistake.

We are getting into the heat now. Fans are going, and the insects (big ones and wee ones) are out in style again. The fan sprays them all over the room! We have got our corn-on-the-cob planted. The pineapples are showing signs of activity, and we should have some by June. There are plenty of bananas in the bazaar, but no oranges.

It is almost eighteen months since we arrived in Assam, and we will not be sorry to see our leave time approaching.

Mum

You would be in bed at night with the fan going, and the insects would hit the fan and be propelled right on to your face. I remember the red ants. They were horrible things. They were bigger than the ordinary ant, and would bite you. It was sore. One time, a whole load of them dug a hole through the bedroom wall, and got in.

Dufflaghur Tea Estate, 1st May 1953

The heat is really making its presence known. The maximum here, is 90 F; but in Calcutta, it was 108 F, two weeks ago. We had the ICI (Imperial Chemical Industries) representative from Calcutta visiting for lunch ten days ago, and he said every blow of wind was roasting hot. I often give the "unda wallah" (egg man) a lift from Halem when I return in the Land Rover on a Friday. This fellow goes forty miles in a bus up to Lakhimpur to buy eggs, and bring them down for us. He charges the Europeans 2½ annas per egg, and the Indians, 2 annas, but he is very good at keeping us supplied during the rains, when transport is very difficult, and eggs are very scarce locally. We use about three or four-dozen weekly, and our own hens cannot keep up with that pace. The eggs are almost half the size of the eggs at home, and one at a time is hopeless.

Mum

I remember the "unda wallah". He was a tall, lanky fellow, and was originally from Afghanistan.

Dufflaghur Tea Estate, 11th May 1953

The recent Comet disaster was a terrible affair (air crash). Three of the passengers were from the neighbouring district, forty miles away. We knew Mrs Pearson quite well, and spent a week in Shillong with her. It is hard to believe that they are completely blotted out. Her husband was a senior superintendent, with only a few years to go. At the various managers' meetings, his opinion was always sought in any ticklish problem. All government regulations are circulated through the Indian Tea Association, and he could quote all circulars, almost to the day, as far back as ten years ago. It is a great pity that a few years of retirement at home, has been denied him, after so many years in Assam. His views will be missed in Calcutta.

There has recently been another crash in India, but we have not seen the newspapers yet. It makes you wonder whether it is really worthwhile travelling by air, when you know that a plane is going to go down every now and then.

We went down to the big district around Tezpur (Thakurbari) for a weekend, two weeks ago. They were giving an amateur performance of "Home at Seven", and did very well indeed. On the way back, we stocked up with cold storage, butter and bacon.

The Morris Oxford is running very well. I have not given it any very hard work. The old Land Rover keeps going, despite everything. We went up the jungle river yesterday, as this will probably be our last chance, since the small bridges (road) are getting washed away. We got sunburned with the increased intensity of the sun.

I crossed the bamboo bridge (Boroi bridge) today after the rain. It is on its last legs. I would not be surprised if it has been breached by tomorrow morning. After that, it takes about seven to ten days for them to get the ferry running.

I've recently done a comprehensive analysis of the various prophylactics in malaria control, and have written my findings regarding circumstances as they are in this district, in a circular to the agents and the Assam Branch of the Ross Institute of Tropical Diseases. Malaria transmission is quite different in different parts of the world and different localities. The modern potent antimalarial drugs (Chloroquine, Camoquin, Daraprim, etc) are very expensive – therefore, not suitable for mass prophylaxis, like Paludrine, which last, unfortunately, has a number of drawbacks.

I always mean to get some photographs of the tea estates and my hospitals. Some of the hospitals are good, whereas others are a bit dilapidated. One or two of my AMOs are very good, but others are practising medicine of twenty years ago. I was surprised at some of the drugs. Some had been discarded as useless, years previously. I am trying to make them aware that medical treatment is undergoing a revolution (a big one too) at the present moment. The advances in every field are terrific. This whole area of mine is very highly malarious (or was) in its foothill situation. The particular mosquito that carries 98% of the malaria here, does not lay eggs in dirty pools, only in clean, slowly, running water, with grassy verges (rivers, streams and very occasionally, rice land).

Mum

The Comet crash was terrible. It put me off flying. I was terrified. Unfortunately, there were not too many options. Even if we took trains and ships, there was always a part of the journey that involved flying. I recall one time we were flying in a cargo plane, carrying full tea boxes. We were with an Indian couple and their children, on our way to Calcutta. Suddenly, the door flew open, and the tea boxes broke loose – although they didn't fall out. Fortunately, neither did we, although everyone was screaming. When we told Arthur Chesshire about this later on, he was shocked, and said we were lucky we hadn't been sucked out.

Dufflaghur Tea Estate, 1st June 1953

We were pleased to get your letters and the cookbook. Reita showed the latter to the cook, and his eyes almost popped out his head with interest. They are always very proud of their calling, and quite prepared for any new tips except, of course, the old ones, who know everything already! Our cook has been with us for nine months now, and is still doing well. Unfortunately, our bearer recently went a bit "off the top storey", shortly after his marriage. His own family are here, and I do not know whether it was the marriage, or his father – but I rather suspect, the latter. He could not get enough money from his son, despite the fact, he was getting everything the poor boy earned. The whole family have now been repatriated to their own country (Central Provinces of India), as the boy was the family's only financial asset. His father was the type to create trouble if the labour force was ever unsettled. Our sweeper has been unfortunate, too. He got drunk one night, and was beaten up by his son – another one, not too stable "on the top". However, the son got more than a "penny lecture" for that from one of the Indian staff.

I have been very busy on malaria statistics, still trying to see which methods are giving the best results at the most economical cost. Dr Gilroy of the Ross Institute has now contacted me, and has asked me to write an article for the India and Pakistan Branch Annual Report. He is going home shortly, and will bring Professor Macdonald from the London headquarters of the Institute back with him for a cold weather tour of Assam, and both will pay us a visit. No one could have been more amazed than I was when the letter arrived! Please take a bow on behalf of your son!! Still, after all the work I have put into it, I will have to go ahead and do more and more! Professor Macdonald was for many years in Assam as a younger man, but now has his headquarters at London University for the branches all over the world. He did the WHO (World Health Organisation) report on malaria conditions in Korea last year – and incidentally, was the man who interviewed me for my present job. The Indian Tea Association pays a regular subscription to the Ross Institute for advice on all matters concerning tropical health. In fact, most of the Assam research is done through the Institute.

The manager of Halem Tea Estate (Guy Heefke) and I were supposed to pay a visit to the practice of one of the greatly experienced tea medical officers, but we have had to postpone this because of the very bad weather conditions. All the cold weather bridges have been washed away with the exceptional amount of rain. We are now about twenty-five inches ahead of last year.

There is to be a Coronation celebration at the Bishnauth Club tomorrow (about thirty to thirty-five miles away). Dr Chesshire is sending his Land Rover to the other side of the Boroi River to collect us. We will go to the river in our own Land Rover, and cross in the small boat. The driver will bring my vehicle back to the bungalow, and come back on Wednesday afternoon to collect us at the river. We have got to know the Chesshires quite well, and will stay overnight with them.

Left to right: Mum and Arthur and Daphne Chesshire

The time has passed very quickly in Assam, and I have never had a minute without needing to do something. Reita has been very good, despite the long hours she has had to spend alone. She always finds something to do. She takes to do with the servants, and I have nothing to do with them now, except meals. The bungalow seems to look after itself, as far as I am concerned. There are a further seventeen months to go before I complete my contract; after that, I will tell you what we are going to do.

Dufflaghur Tea Estate, 24th June 1953

We were very pleased to hear that your own Coronation celebrations ran according to plan. We are now hoping to obtain a film (16mm) for a show at the club, next month. Our own celebrations out here went off quite well. We all went to the neighbouring district for the day, and there was tennis, golf and even stalls, like the "shows" at home. The folks put a considerable amount of work into the preparations, and were rewarded by the pleasure obtained by everyone.

One item, in particular, was very good: "Kiss the Lady". Reita said I was disappointed because it was the lady on the poster, and not the one behind the counter! To win, there was a long piece of bare copper wire, which was twisted into all sorts of shapes, and you had to slip a small loop along it, without touching it, otherwise about half a dozen especially noisy horns were set off at the same time by an electric current, as soon as the wires touched.

I was fascinated by the whole thing, and was among the few people to win a prize, which turned out to be some old tins from the club store that they wanted to get rid of!

We did not get good reception from the BBC that day, and most folks got fed up trying to glue one lug to the radio. Dinner, champagne and a dance went off very nicely in the evening. There was a fireworks display at midnight, but unfortunately, the humidity interfered with some of them.

We were told that the last stragglers did not leave the club until 6am. We stayed what was left of the night with Dr Chesshire, and set off for our own district in the morning.

We have been leading a very quiet life since then, in isolation. The Boroi Bridge was washed away in the middle of May, and I have been fiddling about in small boats every Monday and Tuesday, since then. The delays can be innumerable, and the constancy of it all is very apt to annoy you, when you see everyone fiddling about. No one seems to know the meaning of speed.

We have been very lucky with the heat this year – either that, or we are getting used to it. We make a point of avoiding undue exposure to sunlight, whenever possible. Reita, at any rate, is doing much better this year than last; apart from a few scorching days, I have not felt uncomfortable at all.

The monsoon has now broken properly, with grey rainy days and thunderstorms. It is lovely to hear the rain and feel the temperature drop. The rain we had earlier in the year was due to a fault in the winds over Bengal. The moisture-laden wind from the Bay of Bengal, did not drop its rain because the western component was not strong enough this year (from the opposite direction) to make it do so. All the rain went straight on to Assam (foothills), and almost drowned us out.

The monsoon, however, has now reached us normally. Apart from being about thirty inches of rain ahead of schedule, all is well. East Bengal, in particular, had quite a severe drought before the monsoon arrived.

We were delighted about the results of the Everest expedition, especially when the rumours of failure, owing to the coding system, came out first. It was a pity that some of the less honest types out here decided to distort the facts.

How did you enjoy the TV at the Coronation? We have never seen TV yet. How did "wee" Alex enjoy his "whiff" for tooth extraction? I had to give a "wee whiff" to the five-year old son of the acting manager here, for a very painful molar (first tooth) that was keeping him awake. I was not keen to remove the tooth, as it will be quite a while before he gets a replacement for it, but the pain was disturbing him too much. He did very nicely.

I've removed literally hundreds of teeth since I came out. It is a mixed blessing, especially as I find great difficulty in doing even a fraction of the things that I would like to do at present. The medical officer always gets the name of having little to do out here, and I suppose that is true with some of the old boys. I, however, have succeeded in involving myself in all sorts of things – and I do not hesitate to let them know about it, either!

Reita was counting up the months, the other day. After another one year and four months, our contract will have been completed. If they make it interesting, we will probably renew it, as I cannot see myself getting a decent practice of my own, until I have been at least ten years qualified (1957).

Thank you very much for attending to the BMA subscription. We are getting our newspapers. Reita will be pleased to receive "My Home". How did Pop spend his win on the "Pools"? Two fish suppers?! I have just sent a spool to Calcutta, and will let you have more photographs quite soon.

Mum

Well, "wee" Alex is not so "wee", now. He's my nephew. Willie's son. I remember Queen Elizabeth's Coronation celebrations. The tea planters at Bishnauth also put on a show. One of them came on singing "Some Enchanted Evening", whilst one of the women did a dance. There was food laid on, dancing and a cabaret.

When I got home, I tried to explain in Hindi to our cook what the celebrations were about, and we both ended up getting so mixed up, that he thought the Queen was coming to stay with us!

Everest is another good memory. Allan and I were standing at the River Boroi, waiting to cross to Bishnauth for the celebrations. Smiler and Bridget Russell arrived a short time later to cross as well, and they told us that Everest had been conquered.

We were all so happy, we began to dance! When we got the Calcutta newspapers, it said that it was Tenzing, and not Hilary, who was the first to reach the top.

Left to right: Angus, Bridget and Smiler – and Mum

8

JULY TO SEPTEMBER 1953

Dufflaghur Tea Estate, 15th July 1953

We had intended to make the journey to Tezpur today. One of the assistant managers in the district took a very bad attack of malaria, following influenza, about three weeks ago. He is not a young man – over fifty. His condition was very weak, and his heart not too good, afterwards. I had arranged for him to fly to Calcutta from Tezpur for special investigations, and was going to take him in my Land Rover. Unfortunately, the rain has been so heavy, and the river so high and rough, that it has been impossible for vehicles to cross for a few days.

I got arrangements made, yesterday, for a car to meet him on the other side of the river. I took him down, crossed in the small boat with him, and saw him and his wife into the car. He is a lot better, but I would like investigations before allowing him to resume work.

I hope the Tezpur plane will be able to fly today, as it is most uncomfortable to spend a night there, at this time of year. There are no fans or baths. The only place to stay is the "flat", which is a small river steamer, without an engine, and acts as a quay owing to the variable levels of the river. There are one or two cabins on board, which provide the only reasonable accommodation. Hotels do not exist, unless you are in Calcutta, Shillong, etc. It is quite amusing to see all the floating quays against the bank at all the steamer stopping places.

Life out here goes on very much as usual. We are completely isolated – and to crown it all, one of the resistances in our wireless has burned out, and we cannot even get the "News" or a song! I meant to take it to Tezpur today, but will have to make other arrangements.

I hope to have my report for the Ross Institute completed within the next two weeks. Professor Macdonald was on the list of Coronation Honours (CMG). I thought he would have received a knighthood, but he will be sure to receive this in a few years.

The tea market has improved greatly during the last few months, as have my linguistic skills. My driver keeps teaching me more and more of the language, whilst we are out in the car. He gave me the name for a metal tube, the other day. The Hindi word is: "pipe", and he would not believe me when I said it was the same in English. Reita had a similar experience with the cook. He told her that the Hindi word for eggs done with milk in the frying pan is: "omelette"!

Mum

I remember the "flat"! We had to stay in it a few times, and there were absolutely no facilities. I seem to remember there was a bucket for the toilet...

Dufflaghur Tea Estate, 1st August 1953

I went to bed with influenza last Friday night (24 July), and did not get up until Sunday (26 July). My temperature did not go above 101 F, and was normal by the Sunday morning. With the heat, however, it left me as weak as can be, and I did not strain myself to work before Wednesday.

A letter arrived on Monday (27 July), asking whether the report (Ross Institute) was complete, as they wished to get everything away to print. I had hoped to be able to write the report over the weekend, but that was not to be. The figures and tables were previously completed, and I started writing on Monday – and wrote through the night. By Tuesday, I was more of a corpse than previously. On looking at it now, however, I am very pleased with what I've written, and could not have done it better without "flu".

I've had another letter, wondering when I will be able to pay a visit (with the manager, Guy Heefke, of Halem Tea Estate) to the practice of one of their medical officers in Dooars, West Bengal. I had to postpone this trip previously, but am looking forward to it at the end of August, or beginning of September. We will go via Calcutta, and Reita can get some shopping done. We need a break, in any case.

Guy Heefke, manager of Halem Tea Estate

This old chap (Dr Hay Arthur) in Dooars should be very interesting. He has done a lot of work on malaria control, and was doing some trials of mosquito destruction alone (DDT), without Paludrine prophylaxis, this year. It will be interesting to see what his results have been.

It is a very vast subject, this business of malaria control, where the cost of materials has to be kept constantly in mind. I am trying to evolve a system just now, where I can practically point to the value of every rupee spent, and avoid extravagance. Double the amount of money could easily be spent, which would give half the results, if wrongly applied. I'm hoping that Professor Macdonald will give some financial and professional assistance, through the Ross Institute, to do a little research on some of the very potent, new and expensive anti-malarial drugs in this district. I could talk about malaria for a fortnight, without repeating myself once!

We had no rain for three days, and everything became very hot, indeed. We will be pleased to see some rain and clouds to protect us from the fierceness of the sun. The fans are blaring away all the time. If you go out of reach of a fan for two minutes, you become covered in perspiration. When I come back from work, my shirt and pants (just now) are as though they had been dipped in water and wrung out – only very slightly.

We saw the Coronation film a fortnight ago at the club. It was very inspiring, but I felt a little more descriptive conversation would have helped.

Mum

Allan was a terrible patient! Everything was wrong. Too much self-diagnosis. I remember some of the Coronation film, more particularly, Queen Salote of Tonga, who was riding in an open carriage, with a big smile, waving – all in the pouring rain. Later on, we heard the actual ceremony on a gramophone record.

Dufflaghur Tea Estate, 9th September 1953

We left for Dooars on 27th August. On the way, we were very unfortunate. I got the Land Rover over the river (by ferry) a few days before our departure, in case a last-minute flood would stop us. For a week previously, however, the electrical system started giving trouble, and I got them to give it the "once over" at the factory. On the day of our departure, the Land Rover started missing regularly in one cylinder, and I had to leave it at one of the tea gardens, and borrow the Land Rover from that garden.

We arrived safely in Tezpur, and went to the airfield. We waited up to 6pm, and the freight plane which had been as regular as clockwork during its weekly visits for months previously, did not arrive. When we returned the following day (at 1pm) to see if it might come, the old watchman told us it had arrived fifteen minutes after we left the airfield, and had again called and waited at 6am that morning. We had to rush over to the official passenger airline in Tezpur itself, and went to Gauhati. From there, we took the train overnight, and eventually arrived in a very starved and dirty state at Dr Hay Arthur's bungalow (two days late). They had given up on us by that time, having decided that some of the rivers were uncrossable.

I visited Dr Hay Arthur's practice, and it was well worth the visit. He has a central hospital (with X-ray equipment) and a great organisation, extending out to his smallest dispensary. In my practice, when a patient comes into hospital, he or she brings the husband or wife to act as attendant, and usually half a dozen children have to be put up at the same time. This method is simply asking for a filthy state of affairs. In Dooars, this practice has been eliminated, and only the sick are allowed into hospital. He has trained some of the girls in the labour force to come in for nursing duties and organise the hospitals on lines similar to those at home. These nurses can take a temperature, record it on the chart, give an injection, etc, and the difference can only be described as amazing.

On the way back, we flew down to Calcutta, before flying up to Assam, using a different airway. In Calcutta, I discussed Dr Hay Arthur's set-up with the various agents, and raised many other points. I hope to get a training scheme started during the coming cold weather. These schemes can meet with considerable local opposition, and Dr Hay Arthur tells me that he had to fight for his present set-up, inch by inch. However, I have managed to obtain support from Calcutta, and will push it to its fullest. I have never met a land where respect is only given by the power of your push. However, when in Rome, do as the Romans do.

I only discussed medical services with them, and made no mention of leave in 1954. I was speaking to one of the "chief men", and he did not ask if I might be prepared to renew my contract. Do not be surprised if they give me the sack! I believe that is what they did in the past if the manager considered the medical officer wanted too much done for medical services. Fortunately, European medical officers are at a premium, at the moment.

When we were in Calcutta, we met a young Edinburgh couple, who came out on the ship with us. He is with the British Oil Company in Calcutta. This company works almost entirely in Assam and Pakistan now. We were delighted to see them. His wife was nursing in Edinburgh, and is a Skye girl. They have a small girl of eighteen months, and are flying up to Assam at the end of this month to spend their annual local leave (a fortnight) with us. Dunbar is the name. Reita is looking forward to their visit very much. She sometimes gets a wee bit fed up when I am out of the house a lot. I will run down to Tezpur in the Land Rover, and collect them at the airfield.

We also met a Mr and Mrs McKellar from Renfrew, who came out on the "Batory" with us. Mrs McKellar had been home for almost a year, as her husband was out in the jungle, preparing sites for oil.

Unfortunately, our stay in Calcutta was very short. We arrived at midday on Tuesday, and had to fly up first thing on Sunday morning. We had lots of shopping to do, but I did not manage to do very much by the time I had visited the various offices, had my teeth attended to and gone to some of the garages for spare parts – for the cars, not my teeth! Reita's feet were swollen by the time she had gone round some of the shops, and she gave up in disgust. We did not have much of an appetite in Calcutta, due to rush, lack of sleep and over-chlorinated water. Fortunately, we had been eating like horses in Dooars. Dr and Mrs Hay were very kind to us, and the educational value was terrific.

The vacancy at Tezpur has been given to an old medical officer (Colonel Logan), who ran this practice (Dufflaghur) for three years, up to 1949. He retired after that, but (as I think I said before) he returned. He left some very careful and comprehensive records for the short time he was here before. I will probably give him a call during the cold weather, when we are collecting stores in Tezpur.

Mum

Dr Hay Arthur and his wife were very good to us, and made us feel very welcome. I remember they had a thatched roof on their bungalow, inside which, an iguana had taken up residence. The

Dunbars' little girl was called Fiona. I remember this, because they had an Indian friend who could not say "Fiona", but called her "Piano" instead.

Dufflaghur Tea Estate, 13th September 1953

I have completed my investigations for the Ross Institute, and will be seeing my report in print, in the near future. I am hoping to do another survey during the cold weather of this year, and will have it completed after the New Year, when all the figures for this year are available. In this country, it is possible to obtain malaria control to a very effective degree on the tea garden, probably about 90%. Unfortunately, there is always encroachment of infected mosquitoes from the uncontrolled village areas round about. It is not financially possible to do the whole area "en masse". For that reason, measures for control must always be kept active on the tea estates. There is a certain amount of money that can be spent effectively on estates, and no increase in amount will help, unless the villages are taken into the control programme – but this is not economically possible.

I have been trying to work out what aspects of control are giving a good return and require further development, and which ones could be restricted without any deterioration in our figures. This year promises to be the best on record, but nature has had a considerable part to play in this state of affairs. The particular mosquito, which carries malaria in Assam, would never dream of laying eggs in dirty pools or in tin cans, as happens in parts of Africa. Most of the breeding occurs in grassy streams and clean seepage areas. When the monsoon broke six weeks earlier than normal this year, it washed out all the breeding places during the period when the mosquito population is usually becoming established, and this setback helped considerably in our present year's results.

At the rate these ladies lay eggs, one mosquito killed in May is worth ten thousand in August (probably). I am hoping to concentrate on larval control methods next year, during April and May, to see if we can get the same result without the help of nature. This is interesting, in that larval control has been given a very secondary place in modern malaria control. I will take this up with Professor

Macdonald when he comes in the cold weather, and obtain his advice. I hope to have convincing evidence for him by then.

It is also interesting that the good results obtained this year were obtained with only half of the previous adult doses of Paludrine – a saving of not far short of £1,000 in my district. Children, in whom the disease is liable to be rapidly fatal from high temperature, convulsions, etc, however, were given the previous standard dose. The other main method is to spray the inside of houses with DDT and BHC, so that when mosquitoes come into the houses for a blood meal, they will land on the walls and absorb a lethal dose – and die within twenty-four hours, probably in the jungle. After sucking malaria blood, it takes at least ten days, under ideal circumstances, before the mosquito can pass on the infection. The spraying does not usually prevent them from having a "bite", but if they are killed sometime within the ten days, we are quite satisfied. I could go on for weeks on this subject. It is a bee in my bonnet, and Reita is fed up with the word: "malaria".

As I said before, Dr Hay Arthur (in the Dooars) was very interesting. His methods are worked out to the last degree, especially his laboratory facilities. I am hoping to push the point gradually. My main difficulty is lack of staff to stem the hundreds of blood films, which are required. He has a special man on every tea estate for this purpose, someone who is trained at his central hospital for a few months.

We have got our wireless into commission again. We got a new resistance, and some of the valves were replaced. The set was serviced to clean out corrosion and remove all the insects. It is working well now, and it is a great boon to hear the "News" and "World Affairs".

We had a very dry month in August this year, and it was very hot. The malaria rates were rising by the end of the month. During the last week, however, we have not had a dry day, and the temperature has come right down, for the sun has not been able to get through the layer of clouds. The river was uncrossable for three or four days following our return, except by the small boat.

I forgot to tell you that I grew a beard from Coronation Day for two months. Reita got so used to seeing me with a hairy face that she laughed solidly for an hour after I shaved it off – but she is getting used to my new appearance again.

Dad with a beard

Mum

I liked Allan with a beard. It was blondie-ginger, but he never grew it again. He always had a moustache, though.

9

OCTOBER TO DECEMBER 1953

Dufflaghur Tea Estate, 17th October 1953

Life is going on very much as usual. This has been an unfortunate day for Reita. The cook went to bed with flu yesterday, and as this is one of the religious celebrations, the others have been nipping off, whenever possible. Two of the other servants were off with flu, and came back today. The thought of cooking meals in the heat, under primitive conditions, almost made Reita ill. However, she managed to borrow the acting manager's bearer for a couple of days, and he is able to do straightforward cooking.

We have not made any arrangements for local leave yet. Professor Macdonald and Dr Gilroy are coming to stay two nights with us, near the beginning of November. We are highly delighted and highly honoured about this. It will be a great opportunity to obtain advice on some of our local problems. I am working on some statistics just now, and hope to have some interesting figures available for them.

It will not be long until we are due home leave. It is just over two years since we left Glasgow (14 October 1951). I do not know whether we will be returning to Assam, or not. The life out here has been very isolated, especially for Reita, who does not have her job to keep her interest alive. She says it is impossible to be interested in the home, as she was in Scotland.

I was out attending a couple (they had influenza). They had just returned from home leave, and they are being transferred to another larger tea district, for which, they were very pleased. They said this was the jungliest district they had ever been in. However, if the Company has a vacancy in a better district, and the financial side is good, we will no doubt reconsider our views. If not, we will think about the oils, tin or copper mines in India or West Africa, where there will be a reasonable colony of European employees. I will ask Professor Macdonald about this when he comes to visit us, as he has recently returned from a tour of British concerns in West Africa.

We have been getting on with our vegetable garden this week. The gardeners planted some cabbages and cauliflowers in boxes, a few weeks ago, but it is not possible to plant out anything until all the heavy rain is finished. Since then, we have been getting the peas, beans, beets and turnips into the ground, and should have the vegetable garden completed very soon. We are looking forward to vegetables on the plate.

We are able to get fish now that the turbulent waters have settled a bit, and it is a great change from the old goat. We have had a bit of beef, once or twice, but I am quite sure that they waited until the cow was ready to die before they killed it.

We have not planted any potatoes in the vegetable garden this year. The last lot were like marbles, and it is not possible to get a particular variety of potato out here. It is all down to luck at the bazaar, and you are sure to get the worst, at the best price. We have a lemon tree in the back garden in a very awkward place, and Reita wanted to get rid of it, but we need the occasional lemon for soufflé. This one is too bitter for any other purpose, and we are always borrowing from one of the other managers, who has a lot of lovely ones for juice. I took a couple of cuttings today, and we planted them in another place. It remains to be seen whether these will take, before we cut the tree down.

All the hens in the labour force houses died a few weeks ago, due to chicken cholera. We were very lucky and did not pick up any infection at all. I saw an outbreak of rinderpest among cattle and buffalo, a few months ago. It was knocking the animals over – left, right and centre. Quite a fair proportion of them, especially the buffalo, died. They say that this is the world's number one disease of cattle (so far as losses are concerned). I borrowed a very good book on veterinary disease, a while ago, and became very interested, but have not been able to follow it up owing to lack of time.

Our visitors (the Dunbars, whom we met in Calcutta) had to call off their holiday at the last minute. The oil company are importing helicopters, and he had to go over to Bombay to make arrangements for landing, etc.

The weather has now started to cool down in the last few days. The night temperature is down to 70 F, and the day temperature, never over 86 F. This is the best year on record so far as illness of any description is concerned. Nature helped considerably in this respect.

Mum

We loved the vegetables because they were only available for eating for two or three months of the year. The rest of the time, we had to eat out of tins.

Dufflaghur Tea Estate, 23rd November 1953

Life out here has been going on very much as usual. Professor Macdonald and Dr Gilroy are not coming until 7th December now. They will be staying one night only, and leaving by the small company plane on 8th December. The landing strip is right behind our bungalow. It is for small planes only. They will come up from one of the Tezpur practices. We have invited Dr and Mrs Chesshire to come up for the day to meet them.

I have been doing a great deal of work in preparation for their visit, and hope to have some interesting facts ready by that time. I told you my report for the Ross Institute was sent away a few months ago. I have now gathered sufficient facts and conclusions for an even more comprehensive report, by the beginning of 1954. This year, as well as being the healthiest, has had the lowest infant death rates on record for the practice. In addition, the cost has been considerably below that of previous years. However, as I said before, nature helped considerably.

I have drawn up a huge list of problems for discussion with Professor Macdonald and Dr Gilroy. Their expert advice will help me considerably to maintain the present healthy state in this district – and at the same time, greatly reduce the cost.

The weather has definitely changed now. The evenings are cold, but the sun (during the day, as usual) remains fairly strong. We have had fires in the evening since the middle of November. At night, the temperature is well below 60 F. I did not stop antimalarial activity until the night temperature fell below 70 F – the latter half of October. Since then, the changes have been fairly abrupt. Reita feels the cold so much, that she does not know what she will do when we get back home.

We are hoping to start our weekly picnics at the jungle river fairly soon. We always look forward to them, and derive a great deal of pleasure and health from them. The temporary bridge across the big river (Boroi) between the two halves of my practice, was completed last week, almost a month earlier than last year. This is a great asset. We hope to have a permanent bridge by next year – or, the next again.

The domestic front is doing fairly well at the moment, apart from the usual upsets. The last time I wrote, Reita was having a row with the cook. But this is just part of life in India.

I was reading an article in the "Monthly Review", published by the European Association, about the new Calcutta Cemetery, opened in 1777, with quotations from Kipling (Rudyard Kipling) and others, portraying the unhealthy conditions and early deaths from pestilence and disease. Young brides came out and died within a few months. The article bored a hole into me when I considered the present healthy state of affairs, relative to that which previously existed.

The one main problem today, is nutrition and the wherewithal to buy food. I have seen only one case of blackwater fever since I came to Assam – in a child. This was the regular menace only a few years ago. We still get the usual case of typhoid every now and then, but fortunately, we now have the armamentarium to cope effectively with this. Even the food situation in Assam is very much better than in any other part of India.

One of the older tea planters in the district took a very slight stroke in the tea garden, last Thursday. I had to sleep in his bungalow for two nights, until I could get arrangements made to remove him by small plane. I flew with him to the mission hospital at Jorhat, and left him feeling fairly bright and free from personal anxiety. He was fortunate in not having any paralysis at all. He lives by himself, as his wife and family are at home just now. It was the first time I had been in the light plane, and the view of my own bungalow from the air was very impressive.

We went to Tezpur by car today, to collect some stores in preparation for Professor Macdonald's visit on 7th December. We re-plated the batteries on the tea garden, which meant we had to go without electricity at night for a week, and had to use paraffin lamps. Finally, my Land Rover was giving me trouble, so it got an overhaul. I have had it rebarred, so I should have trouble-free driving – at least for a while.

Mum

I remember the tea planter who had a stroke. His name was Freddy Petch. He was the manager of one of the tea gardens. After his stroke, he had to retire.

Dufflaghur Tea Estate, 12th December 1953

We had Professor Macdonald and Dr Gilroy with us on Monday and Tuesday. They were both very nice and gave me a great deal of useful advice regarding malaria control. They were greatly interested in the development of medical services for the practice – a central laboratory, etc. Reita and I hope to spend a few days with Dr Gilroy, during January or February, so that I can see his laboratory and those in some of the practices around Jorhat. My agents have asked me for definite proposals in this matter.

We are going to Shillong on Friday 18th December, and returning about 29th December. It will be cold at this time, but it will be a nice change. We went down to Bishnauth for lunch with Dr and Mrs

Chesshire, yesterday. We were trying to reach an agreement, so that we could put definite proposals to the agents regarding home leave and DTM&H (Diploma in Tropical Medicine and Hygiene) courses. Professor Macdonald was saying that there are two courses annually at London for DTM&H. One course starts in October, and one in March. Each one lasts five months. I am not too keen to come home in the winter, and would prefer to take the March one (1955).

Today, I was doing a bit of operating at Halem. The AMO's child, aged eighteen months, has a harelip, and I managed to put it right. I also saw an interesting and serious obstetric case today (placenta praevia), and got the bleeding stopped. I will try to complete her delivery tomorrow. I have only had one other case like hers, since I came to Assam. The previous case (about five months ago) lost so much blood in the first spurt, that I thought we would never manage to save her. Despite everything, we got her pulled round and delivered.

The birth rate in Assam is more than twice that of Britain. One tea garden in the district succeeded in producing babies at the rate of 59 for every 1,000 of total population, during 1952. The corresponding figure at home is seldom above 18. The death rate in infants, in the first year of life, is the same in proportion. This figure is reckoned to give an indication of the social progress of a community, adequacy of medical treatment, etc. This figure has more than halved itself since modern malaria control was initiated.

One of the assistant managers shot an elephant, a couple of weeks ago. The elephant was trampling through the rice fields (now dry), eating and generally upsetting the crop. The villagers were very worried about it. He went up to the edge of the jungle (just before dark) and managed to get a shot at it with his heavy rifle – a 0.45. The ordinary service rifle is hopelessly inadequate for an elephant. He did not, however, get a very satisfactory shot, and the animal lumbered into the jungle. The next day, he went into the jungle (about 6 miles away) on a tame elephant. He saw where the rogue had fallen over and picked itself up again. There was no blood. The tracks led into a steep-sided streambed, and he did not want to go up it in case the wounded animal charged him. A few days later, however, the villagers discovered the animal, which was in active stages of putrefaction.

I had an amazing adventure, three weeks ago. A cat, belonging to the Halem assistant manager (who was temporarily working on a different tea estate in my district), died. From the history of the fatal illness, it was not possible to exclude the possibility of rabies, and the assistant had been handling the cat during that time. He came to tell me that it had died the previous evening, and had been buried in the back garden. We set off, at once, to dig it up, so that the brain could be sent to Shillong for examination. We dug it up by torchlight (quite an exhumation!), and I chopped its head off, put it into formalin, and sent it off to Shillong. We did not take any chances, and started the course of antirabic injections. The report eventually came back that the head was in advanced stages of putrefaction when it arrived in Shillong, and it was not possible to give any report regarding the absence, or otherwise, of rabies.

Mum

I vaguely remember the incident with the cat, but there was another incident involving a dog. Allan and I were sitting in our bungalow having breakfast, when a dog came in. We knew it belonged to one of the assistant managers, and let it sniff around our legs. A short time later, it died of rabies. Fortunately, it didn't bite either of us.

10

JANUARY TO MARCH 1954

Dufflaghur Tea Estate, 17th January 1954

We made a last-minute decision to spend local leave with the Dunbars in Calcutta (the Edinburgh couple – he works with the Burma Oil Company in Calcutta), and we enjoyed out holiday very much. We hope they will be able to come up and have a holiday with us here, so we can have the opportunity of repaying them.

Poor Reita got a terrific list of shopping from practically everyone in the district, and she says that she would never try to do so much shopping, in such a short time, again. We stayed in Calcutta for only nine days, and returned home two days before the New Year to take part in the annual celebrations at the club.

We had to have a part in the "show", which the district was laying on at Hogmanay. Fortunately, our parts required no rehearsing for there was no dialogue. The club (Halem) was "done up" to represent "Puddleton in the Mud", and the "Reverend Alou Sippets" (potato crisps, when translated) introduced all the members of the Parish. Reita was one of the three little girls from school. Of the other two, one was forty-five, and the other one was pregnant. I represented the village doctor with a bent back, cotton wool beard and hair, a cardboard top hat – and a stethoscope and ear syringe hanging from braces. The "show" was very daft, but seemed to give our visitors quite a bit of amusement.

I have accepted a second contract with the Company for three years, beginning 1st November 1954. By the time we come back from leave, the first year of the contract will have been completed. I will be taking the DTM&H (London) from March 1955, for five months. The Company has agreed to give extended leave with pay for a total of about eight months.

Mum

Allan enjoyed studying and advancing himself in medicine. He was absorbed in the topic of malaria, and did a lot of research.

Dufflaghur Tea Estate, 27th January 1954

Life, socially, has been quite nice since the New Year celebrations. Yesterday was the Republic Day holiday in India, and we went up the jungle river for a picnic. We saw the usual elephant droppings, but nothing more startling than that.

The BMA Annual General Meeting (Assam Branch) takes place between 11th and 14th February, this year. Reita and I are hoping to fly over for about a week, and have the opportunity of visiting the various laboratories around Jorhat, so that I can draw up final proposals for one in this district. I have had official sanction to do so.

Mum

It was quite common to see elephant droppings up at the picnic area. It was a spot the elephants would visit because they liked to walk through the water and bathe in order to cool down.

Dufflaghur Tea Estate, 7th February 1954

Life out here has been very much as usual. We go up the jungle at the weekend, and try to get as much work as possible done during the week. There have been a number of dances and parties at the various clubs round about, so we have been jaunting about a bit more. I have had word from the agents to say that it will be in order for me to go to the Annual General Meeting of the Assam Branch of the BMA, and that I can stay on a day or two longer at Jorhat, to visit laboratories round about. I have already designed a new hospital for Dufflaghur, and apart from some small technical alterations, this is now off to the architects, having been accepted. It will cost between £5,000 and £10,000, plus the extras later.

The egg situation out here is likely to be slightly poor during the hot weather. There was a great epidemic of chicken cholera, which reduced the stocks greatly. In some places, it extinguished it. They will soon build up, however. We have not bought any more birds because of this, and our present stock is getting eaten up – only five left. The vegetables, however, have been a great success this year – more peas, etc, than we know what to do with. Only the tomatoes are late.

I took some photographs of an Indian piper, a few days ago, plus a retinue of orphan boys. They were good performers, and earned their Rs 7/-.

Piper and orphan boys visiting Dufflaghur

Mum

I remember the orphan boys. They were all Indian, with the exception of one, who was white. Their parents had abandoned them at birth, and none had reached their teens. The children were playing the Scottish bagpipes. There was an Indian man with them, supervising. They just appeared from nowhere, and we thoroughly enjoyed the "show".

Dufflaghur Tea Estate, 17th February 1954

We arrived at Jorhat (by air) last Thursday, but had to return home yesterday, as there was no space on the plane for today or tomorrow. We enjoyed meeting the different tea garden doctors, and hearing what they had to say.

BMA Assam Branch AGM (Jorhat) 1954
Dr Gilroy: seated to the left; and Dad: standing to the right

During the meeting, we stayed at the Tocklai Experimental Station, and flitted over to Dr Gilroy's bungalow on Monday morning. He took us round the various laboratories, as well as a number of the good tea garden hospitals within an area of fifty to sixty miles. It was very interesting, and gave me plenty of good ideas. Dr Gilroy, himself, was like a breath of inspiration. He could solve all my problems in two minutes. He has done a terrific amount of research into problems affecting tropical countries, both here and Africa, when he served with the Colonial Medical Service, and was awarded the OBE. I have now got a very clear picture of what is required here. With such expert backing, it gives me a fairly free hand to get things done, otherwise I would have to go to great lengths, writing and explaining things, before anything would move.

We met a Glasgow doctor (Poole) and his wife, and had lunch with them on Monday, while we were touring around. He qualified at the beginning of 1945, and had been in the same flat at the Royal Infirmary as I was.

While we were in Jorhat, we went along, one evening, to the Scottish minister's house (Mr and Mrs Nelson) for an evening of country dancing. They are going to stay with us when they come over for a service, probably in six to eight weeks.

I was talking to the Roman Catholic priest today. He is doing his regular visit to the Roman Catholic communities among the labour force. These chaps often sleep in mud huts when they are doing their rounds, and eventually take malaria, dysenteries, etc. I do not know how they manage to keep going. He was Italian, and had been home only once in twenty-eight years, and had almost forgotten his own language.

Mum

Dr Gilroy was Australian. He had spent time in Papua New Guinea, doing research. His wife was also Australian. I remember Dr Poole and his wife from Glasgow. I also remember the Nelsons. We saw them on quite a few occasions when we were in Assam, and remained in contact after returning home.

Dufflaghur Tea Estate, 1st March 1954

I received a report from Professor Macdonald, which gave his opinion of medical conditions out here. He also said that if I kept on working the way I have been, I should be able to convert this into one of the good practices in Assam, but that I would have to start from scratch, and there was plenty work involved.

I get a bit fed up at times, trying to point out the obvious to people, who do not want to see; however, I have got the ball rolling, slowly, and feel quite sure that with plenty of pushing, it will continue to do so. I have got the plans for the central laboratory completed, and these will be sent out for estimates. It is probably going to cost about £1,500 to £2,000 to get it functioning, and the agents have accepted this, in principle.

Dr Gilroy has promised to come over during the monsoon to advise me on medical matters, generally. I have started preparing for the DTM&H course next year. Last week, I started taking the book round in the car with me, and have been making steady progress. I hate to waste hours and hours, each week, on driving. My driver is a good chap and very honest. If he forgets to do something, he admits it, gets the row, and then gets on with the job.

Today, the old sweeper came on duty in an inebriated condition. As a matter of policy, I will have to give him a "telling off", and threaten to cut his pay, etc. I did not have time today, as I have two European patients at the opposite end of the practice, both convalescing from dysentery, and had to go out there after doing my normal rounds.

Mum

Poor Puto, the sweeper, was probably nearly fifty. He belonged to the lowest Indian caste – and in accordance with the system, had the lowest job (sweeping the floors and cleaning the toilets). He was always sweeping away with something like the branch of a tree, whether anything needed sweeping or not. He got on with his work, and didn't say very much.

Dufflaghur Tea Estate, 15th March 1954

I delivered a baby today, at 2½lbs. We have great difficulty with our premature babies. The mothers refuse to understand that a small thing, making feeble efforts to suck, might be getting nothing. However, we strive away, and our results get better each year. Artificial feeding is not possible, unless for exceptional cases, for economic reasons.

Ten years ago, over 15% of all infants born died within one year of birth. Even as recently as 1949, the figure was 12%. We have now managed, during 1953, to get it down to 7½%, and with our increasing effort – and facilities – hope to take it down to 5%. The corresponding figure in Britain, varies between 1½% to 2½%. I always watch this figure closely, as it is taken to give an indication of the adequacy of medical facilities, treatment and social progress of a community.

I got some strawberry plants from one of the managers, and hope to get some cuttings. They do not produce anything during the hot weather; however, when the cold weather comes, they start to produce fruit – usually about January.

I had a long talk (at Halem) with one of the London directors of McLeod Russel. As a tea agency, they are very interested in medical matters. Some of the agencies are starting a scheme to give their managers four months leave after every eighteen months of duty, and the local managers are very pleased with this arrangement. It will make a big difference to those who have children at school, and those whose wives are not able to be out here all the time for domestic reasons.

The assistant manager at Halem Tea Estate told me that he was out shooting, when he noticed a trip wire across a jungle path. When he investigated, he found a trap with a huge bow and arrow, ready to go off. It was one of the Duffla traps for killing wild buffalo for food.

The Dufflas are a jungle tribe, who come down to the bazaars, every now and then, to buy salt and other tit-bits. The assistant manager had a terrible row with them about the trap, and made one of them go around with him to avoid the traps. It is always poisoned arrows they use, and they can put a huge buffalo on its back within minutes. They are a curious crowd of people. They do not cut their hair, but roll it up in a ball at the front, and put a piece of bamboo – like a knitting needle – straight through it. This is to attract and keep a good spirit inside the ball of their hair. Their complexion is much fairer than that of the tea garden labourer.

Duffla with his son in front of Dad's Land Rover

I always intend to buy a gun to shoot the jungle "murghi" (wild fowl), but never seem to have the time. I will bring back a twelve bore after home leave. I have no desire to shoot tigers.

On Thursday, we are going to a party in the neighbouring district. It will probably finish early the following morning, before the dawn breaks. The party spirit will soon quieten down when the weather gets warmer. Everything just now is very dirty, and the winds are lifting dust off the road. It is impossible to go out without being covered with a layer of dust on your return. We will probably get a shower of rain fairly soon to clear the atmosphere. This will create difficulty too, as the bridges (on the roads) are under repair just now, and the detours will be muddy.

Mum

That damned gun! His mother must have put him right on that one, because he didn't bring a gun back after our home leave – at least, I never saw one!

I remember the Dufflas well. Some of them used to come down to the bungalow looking for cigarettes and medical attention – which they got. They would smoke a cigarette and catch the ash with the other hand, and when they'd finished smoking the cigarette, they would eat the ash. They spoke their own language, and whenever we tried to fix a time for them to return for treatment, they would point to the sky, and indicate that that would be where the sun would be positioned. When they returned, the sun would be exactly there.

I remember one occasion when Allan and I were up at the picnic area alone. On the other side of the river, there was a group of Dufflas, and they took knives out to sharpen. We didn't know if they were doing it out of mischief, or for any other reason, but since we'd never seen them do it before, we didn't want to take any chances, so we upped and went, scrambling up rocks, making a hasty retreat!

Dufflaghur Tea Estate, 24th March 1954

We had quite a sharp earthquake tremor on Monday morning (6am), which lasted for more than a minute. We got out of bed and on to the front lawn as quickly as we could in our night attire – and bare feet. Bottles were knocked off shelves. Nothing was broken, but there were some big cracks in the plaster. The whole surface of the earth kept tilting back and forward, and it looked so peculiar to see the electricity poles slanting first one way, and then the other.

Our type of earthquake is not volcanic in origin. The Himalayan Mountains are very recent, relative to the likes of the Alps. As the centre of the earth is constantly shrinking, the surface crust eventually falls in slightly, and in doing so, produces a terrific shudder for hundreds of miles around the main centre. Flooding caused the main damage during the last earthquake. Rivers in the hills got blocked by landslides, and eventually broke through and came thundering down into the valley. We are fortunate in not having any large rivers within five to six miles of the bungalow.

When we were going up to the jungle picnic place on Sunday, a female leopard crossed the road about ten yards in front of us. She probably could not work out what we were. We eventually drove on, and left her to stare after us. Some of the keen sportsmen were saying they had never had the opportunity of meeting a leopard on that road during the day. Just as well – for the leopard!

Mum

I remember that particular earthquake. It was daylight. There were flashes coming from the electricity poles as they swayed – and the ground was moving. But I was more distressed by the fact my nightdress was on inside out, and I didn't want to be found dead like that!

11

APRIL TO JUNE 1954

Dufflaghur Tea Estate, 16th April 1954

We have had over ten inches of rain. The grass has turned green again, and the tea bushes are throwing out leaf. The rain has kept the temperature from going up, as it normally does at this time of year. After the rain stops, it will turn hot very suddenly, and the plucking will be in full swing. They have already started manufacturing tea, but not in any great quantity.

On Tuesday, about 9pm, a sudden terrific wind arose, and slammed doors and windows with its force. Many of the labourers' houses were blown over, and branches were blown off shade trees – and the same damage was done to tea bushes. The steel door between our bedroom and bathroom, got completely jammed, and we had to get a man over to loosen the steel frame to get it open again. The roads have been very bad again, and many people have been getting stuck in the fresh soil (thrown on the road to maintain height) because it did not have the time to settle before the arrival of the rain.

I always seem to be kept very busy. If my temperament were different, I could probably overlook a great deal and jog on, as many have done before me, but I am just not made that way.

The Chairman of the Assam Branch of the Indian Tea Association came with Dr Chesshire (from the neighbouring practice) ten days ago, by light plane, to discuss hospitals in regard to Government regulations. We got quite a surprise when the plane came down, and they made their way over to the bungalow.

I had a letter from Professor Macdonald, who has returned to England. He said he hoped to see Dr Gilroy and me when we were in London, as he did not expect to visit India again for some time. Dr Gilroy has said that he will pay a visit to the practice during the present year. They are a great help in the solution of local problems.

We have been very lazy with our entertainment programme during the cold weather, and will have to invite everyone at the last minute. We have arranged a dinner for nine, tonight. Reita is running about doing last minute inspections, and giving orders to the servants. She cannot tolerate anything, unless it is just right, and our poor servants do not have much of a clue. Still, it is amazing how well they rise to the occasion. Unfortunately, we had to sack our night watchman. He had been drinking heavily, and kept falling asleep every night. On the occasion in question, he fell asleep before we had finished dinner in the evening, and we felt this was just too much.

Dufflaghur Tea Estate, 9th May 1954

I have had another spell where everything comes on at once, and I just cannot cope with it all. I also had recurrent diarrhoea for a week, but did not find any evidence of amoebic dysentery. It has almost cleared up with treatment, however, and I am now feeling absolutely fine. One is always liable to that in this land. The wife of one of the managers had amoebic dysentery, a few weeks ago, and I had to organise very thorough treatment in order to get her bowel completely clear. She did not wish to go to Shillong, and her condition is now excellent.

There are three expectant mothers (Europeans) in the practice at the present moment, which is unusual for the small number of Europeans. They are all doing fine, however, and will be sent up to the hills (Shillong) for their babies, as it is far too hot here, during the rains.

We had the Scottish minister from Jorhat (Mr Nelson) staying with us last weekend, and had a service in the club on Sunday evening. He was very nice, and had excellent stories to tell us, having been in India since the end of the war – and also in Indo-China, Borneo and many other places. Mrs Nelson did not come with him as she is an expectant mother, and wanted to stay at home.

We are having the first film of the Queen's tour (16mm) at the club (Halem) tomorrow evening, and we are looking forward to it.

Everyone is busy at the present moment, as the growth of leaf is getting heavier every day. We have had some very hot days, but the temperature on the whole, has been much below the average for this month, owing to excessive amounts of rain during April and this month. The poor Calcutta people were having up to 110 F before they got a Nor-Wester to cool things down. We have seldom had 90 F, but will no doubt suffer for it in August, like last year, when it was dry and hot.

The agents have asked me to prepare a report, incorporating the figures in this district (malaria and general sickness) for publication (private) through the Indian Tea Association, and for circulation to tea gardens in north-east India. You could have knocked me over when the letter arrived! One of the managers was quibbling about malaria policy, so I wrote a letter showing our previous results, cost, etc, and what we had to gain by accepting the expert advice of Professor Macdonald and Dr Gilroy. I will have to get Dr Gilroy to read it, after preparation, so that I can get his advice. I do not get much trouble nowadays in regard to medical policy, as most of the managers are only too anxious to get the best possible results.

Mum

Allan was always getting diarrhoea because of the conditions he worked in, and close contact with his patients – also not being able to wash his hands properly. He was always very particular about hygiene, but the hospitals on the tea gardens were very primitive, which is why he was so keen to progress with his plans for a new hospital and laboratories.

Dufflaghur Tea Estate, 28th May 1954

The weather has been very hot and wet, but we are used to that. The cold weather bridge (over the Boroi), which separates the two halves of the practice, was washed away two days ago. As before, this will give transport troubles and time wastage for another six months. I have decided to stay one night per week on the other side of the river, this year, to make the work easier. Reita can stay that night with the Pattullos, who kindly offered to put her up.

The malaria season is now firmly established. This keeps me on the run, as there is always somebody making mistakes over the control measures, or somebody trying to economise behind my back, which can be so exasperating when we have the armamentarium to keep the disease completely suppressed. However, enough said about that!

Dr Gilroy of the Ross Institute is coming over for a few days (during the monsoon) to give me his suggestions and help. This will be good for the report I am preparing for the ITA (Indian Tea Association). I am getting plenty of bouquets at the moment, but you can bet your boots, this will be followed by bricks! Such is life.

We lost all our hens to chicken cholera last week. One died daily, until the whole six of them were gone. They weren't laying very well, in any case. The Pattullos lost a cow from anthrax, however, none of the others have picked up the infection – so we hope.

Mum

I remember the chicken cholera! It was the man we bought the eggs from, who caused that. He'd been selling us rotten eggs, and to make up for it, brought us a chicken – and that chicken had the cholera!

Dufflaghur Tea Estate, 13th June 1954

Two days ago, a telegram arrived from the agents to ask when we wanted to arrive in England. I have said 12th February 1955, at the latest. This will give us a wee while at home, before going to London. Reita reckons that we will be sailing on the "Caledonia", leaving

Bombay on 19th January 1955. We will have our official booking very soon now. The time should slip past very quickly.

We are thinking about going to one of the holiday resorts at the Bay of Bengal for two weeks in October (1954), as we will be due local leave this year. I have not sent any more tea as there are a lot of declaration forms to be filled in, and nobody is showing any enthusiasm to help me out – as one soldier said to the other! The prices of tea at the present moment, are beyond all expectation. I hope it will last for a wee while, as the agents have almost agreed to build me a laboratory, and supply me with some central staff for the practice. This would be a great help. I still seem to be kept very busy, and I cannot catch up with all the jobs I have undertaken.

We have had about four and a half inches of rain during the last three days, and the roads are flooded at all the weak spots. There will be plenty of trouble at the river crossing tomorrow morning. Reita is going over to stay the night with me on the other side. The mail buses have not been able to cross for three days, so we will get a big pile of mail when the water level falls.

12

JULY TO SEPTEMBER 1954

Dufflaghur Tea Estate, 5th July 1954

We were pleased to receive your letters. When you said that June had been a cold month, we could hardly visualise it. We have been lucky with temperatures this year, except last week; the blanket of clouds, which was protecting us, cleared up, and the sun has been scorching down on us, since. I notice the heat most when I am crossing the river to the other section of the practice, and today, it was very hot.

They are still talking of building a permanent bridge, and hope to start this year. That would be the best help anyone could give towards my own personal convenience in running this practice. I have started taking "tiffin" (midday meal) on the other side of the river, on Mondays and Thursdays. Staying overnight simply wasted time.

Last week, three buses got bogged in the sand at the river crossing when the water was high, and had to be lifted out and dragged by two elephants when the water level eventually went down, this week.

We received a letter from the agents stating that we have been booked on the "Caledonia", leaving Bombay on 19th January (1955). The Anchor Line boats are two days slower than P&O, but are reputed to be much more comfortable. They take about twenty-one days. We will probably arrive in Liverpool on 8th February, and can then make our way north. At the moment, I am thinking of going into "digs" in London, so that Reita can have a longer holiday with her own folks. The University or Tropical School, should be able to help me in this matter, unless you can get Pop persuaded to live in London for a while, to make it worthwhile looking for furnished accommodation.

I have almost completed my arrangements for registration at the Tropical School, and would be pleased and grateful if Pop would send the enclosed registration form, along with a cheque for £42, to the following address: The Financial Officer, London School of Hygiene and Tropical Medicine, Keppel Street, Gower Street, London WC1. The cheque should be made payable to: "The London School of Hygiene and Tropical Medicine". I would like him to pay the complete £42 now, otherwise they might not retain a place for me, and I would have to go to London before the beginning of the course to complete all the registration particulars. I will square it up with Pop when I get home.

Tell him, if he wants to go to London, he will have to take his own blankets with him! That might encourage him. He would be able to see all the London gardens, docks, Madame Tussaud's, Tower of London, etc. He could take a trip down to Brighton for the day, go to the pictures, visit the Department of Agriculture, research stations, etc.

Dufflaghur Tea Estate, 3rd August 1954

We are looking forward to our leave. Reita will probably go straight on to Islay, and I will go straight to Dumbarton (*where Dad's parents moved to on their retiral*). She will then come back in order to go down to London, but we have no definite plans yet. We are getting it very hot just now.

Until a week ago, it rained every day, and the roads are in a terrible mess. Without the Land Rover, I could not have managed to get out to work on many occasions during July. We were astonished to hear "Assam" on the "BBC News", a couple of days ago. The mail buses and other vehicles have not been able to cross the Boroi River for about two weeks, owing to the very high level of the river, with tree trunks roaring down in the current. When I crossed today, it had decreased to a very small river again, but sandbanks had been deposited on one side, about fifty yards wide, and they were preparing a wire so that vehicles would be able to cross it. The sand was still soft today, and my legs were sinking up to the knees, trying to cross it at some parts.

The terrific force of the monsoon rain carries everything before it, including sand and soil. We had almost thirty inches of rain during July, and will probably have a hot August to compensate for it. There was an elephant on the river today, clearing away the ragged tree trunks to guard against possible damage to the boats. The "Ghat Babu" (ferry controller) was saying that it costs Rs 25/- a day for a big elephant to carry out this type of work.

Life goes on pretty much as usual. The Pattullos are doing fine. Dr Gilroy of the Ross Institute has promised to come over and see the practice for a few days. I hope he will manage this month, before the malaria season starts to decrease.

The wife of the Indian manager of a neighbouring garden slipped on the floor and broke her ankle, a few weeks ago. Fortunately, because we got two dry days, the airstrip dried out sufficiently for the small plane to land. She went over the river to Jorhat, had her X-ray and plaster applied at the mission hospital, and was back again within four hours. That evening, the rain came down in buckets, and the strip was useless for more than a week. They are now talking about an "all weather" strip for the area.

My Land Rover is now beginning to give me a bit of trouble. Nothing serious, but it is always needing spare parts. I hope the agents will give me a new one when I come back from leave. It has been a lot of hard work on very bad roads. My Morris Oxford has not been much good to me for the last few weeks.

The "dhan" (rice) crop has now been planted (I should say, transplanted) from the "kutipans" (original beds). It will have another six weeks of flooding, and will then go dry like wheat, and be harvested in December. The early paddy (rice field) was harvested during July.

Dufflaghur Tea Estate, 23rd August 1954

Reita had neuralgia from a very bad lower molar tooth, which had to be removed. It was quite an operation! She "made off" to the Pattullos' bungalow – and after the extraction, she had quite a bit of "after pain" owing to some infection in the socket. This is now completely healed, and she is feeling much better.

I did not manage to get over the river today, owing to the terrific downpour of rain over the weekend. I will probably manage all right tomorrow, as the water level falls as quickly as it rises. We have not had an uncomfortable monsoon this year at all, and we have very little time left for extreme heat. I think this is partly because of the heavy rain, dull skies and acclimatisation.

The prices of tea at the present moment, I believe are better than they have been. The managers out here, are very pleased, as this means they will be getting good commission.

Mum

I remember getting my tooth out very well indeed. Every time Allan tried to operate, I kept hold of Pat Pattullo, the manager. Eventually, Allan managed to jag my mouth with something and pull the tooth out.

Dufflaghur Tea Estate, 19th September 1954

We were very pleased to receive your letters, and hope you are gaining your strength again. I remembered your birthday (Mother) when I last wrote, but had already sealed the letter. Please accept our very best regards. I cannot remember whether you were thirty years of age, or sixty on 9th September...

We are doing well. The worst of the heat is now behind us, but we still have the fans ticking over. We will need a fire in the evening, within another three or four weeks. Reita has knitted me a pullover, and is now completing a cardigan to keep me warm. The icicles will be dangling from our noses when we arrive in Liverpool, but I do not think even that will dampen our enthusiasm.

Mrs Nelson (the Scottish minister's wife) paid a visit to Assam, a week or so ago, to inspect the flood damage. Dibrugarh and some other areas on the south bank of the Brahmaputra have been badly eroded by the floods. We are much more fortunate on the north bank. Being next to the foothills, the streams and rivers are flowing too fast, and are not able to deposit a serious amount of sandy silt.

After the floods in other areas, all vegetation has been covered by one or two feet of sand, after the floodwater drained away. This silting action is probably one of the biggest problems created by tropical rivers. They fill themselves up with sand until the bottom of the river is almost level with the bank, and then flood over until they have created a completely new river bed. The Brahmaputra, at the present moment, is more than five miles wide, and the channels keep changing all the time. Mrs Nelson said that the Central Government would be willing to help to the extent of 50%, or even more, in regard to the cost of development schemes, but that the provincial governments must help themselves. The ferry agent (at the Boroi River) was telling me that a permanent bridge will be built within two or three years. My feet will be well washed by then!

I am now beginning to get all my business cleared up in preparation for our departure. We will need vaccination and cholera inoculation certificates, income tax clearance certificates, customs clearance, travellers' letters of credit, tickets, etc. It will not be very difficult, however, as I know exactly what is required this time, and I will not be fishing about in the dark. We will probably leave the tea garden about 13th or 14th January.

Dufflaghur Tea Estate, 20th September 1954

When I was across the river today, the water level was completely down. A week ago, it was a raging torrent, and a lorry, which had got stuck on the dry sandbank, was almost completely covered. This was the fourth vehicle, during the year, to be cut off and covered by the rising level of the river. Fortunately, all were pulled out without too much difficulty.

13

OCTOBER TO DECEMBER 1954

Dufflaghur Tea Estate, 20th October 1954

The "maalis" (gardeners) have started to plant the cold weather seeds, which are supplied from Calcutta. Our strawberries, which we got from an enthusiastic gardening assistant, are shooting out runners, left, right and centre. By the time we come back from leave, we should be able to expect a fairly good crop. Unfortunately, they say that the taste is very disappointing in comparison to strawberries at home. I put some lemon and orange tree cuttings into the garden about ten days ago, and they have all taken nicely. They are a good variety and not jungly, like most of the ones available. One of the managers cut them for me from his garden. I see Reita out supervising the "maalis", making sure the place is tidy. All the vegetables and flower seeds are planted, but we will not be able to get much use of them this year.

I have not heard whether a locum will be taking over during my leave absence, or whether Dr Chesshire will be running the two practices. Reita is knitting away. She has finished the cardigan, and is knitting a twin-set for herself. We will probably need plenty of clothing when we arrive in Liverpool. I hope the dock strikes will not upset the shipping schedules.

We are getting the newspapers you send regularly, now that the flooding has stopped. I believe the railway line is still breached at three rivers, and that it will be many months before it is back to normal again. They have been carrying the mail over in small boats at these points, in the same way they do at the Boroi River when it is bad. All letter post, however, comes up by airmail from Calcutta to Tezpur (including our Calcutta paper), and it is only parcel post that is difficult.

Reita has started counting the days now. I was getting a bit browned off a few weeks ago, and longed to be away, but I received a letter from Dr Gilroy to say that he would be coming over for a few days, and this has brightened me up quite considerably. There are so many people who are not even casually interested in creating an interesting medical service for the doctor, that it is a great tonic to hear someone who is interested, and someone who is so able to advise on tricky points.

The temporary bamboo bridge (over the Boroi River) is now nearing completion. In a week or so, at least that difficulty will be behind me.

We have been doing a bit of entertaining recently, getting round all the people, so that there will be no rush at the last minute. Reita says she is going to start washing the curtains on 1st December. She has not been able to get her twin-set finished because of "clearing-up" jobs, but there is not much left to be done of it.

Mum

Allan really did have a problem in getting people interested in his medical projects, but kept pursuing them in the hope that he could improve medical conditions out there. Even when there was more money available, people were reluctant to use any of it for medical development. This upset Allan greatly.

Dufflaghur Tea Estate, 16th November 1954

The Pattullos went up to Shillong a week ago, for local leave. They are doing fine. We have not taken local leave this year, and have no time to do so now. We just can't work up any enthusiasm, with home leave so near. We left it too late to send Christmas cards, so the only thing we will be able to send this year, will be ourselves – a few weeks after Christmas.

We will be leaving the tea garden in seven weeks – lovely thought! Reita is now on the second sleeve of the twin-set, but she thinks the wool is going to run out too quickly, and that she will have to send for another ounce.

Recently, I have seen some jobs advertised in Kuwait in the BMJ, and sometimes think we would be better off in the "oils", where medical facilities are modern.

We will be able to go up the jungle river next weekend, for the first time this season. It will be a nice change to get a swim, but the water by now will be very cold. I hope you have six hot water bottles and half a ton of cotton wool for us when we arrive home!!

Mum

So did I! I did manage to finish the twin-set. In fact, I did a lot of knitting when I was in Assam. I enjoyed it, and it passed the time. Ina Pattullo also did a lot of knitting, and if we weren't playing cards, we were knitting.

Dufflaghur Tea Estate, 19th December 1954

We have fixed up to leave the tea garden on 11th January (1955), and will stay a few days in Calcutta to get all our clearance certificates, etc, in order. Next Saturday will be Christmas, but we cannot work up any enthusiasm with the thought of home leave so soon.

I have been kept very busy recently with sick Europeans (dysentery), and trying to clear up all the odd jobs, which pile up at the last minute. I also had an amputation to do yesterday, and the preparation and sterility for this is very exacting. It takes much more time and energy to supervise the preparation, than it does to do the actual job. The poor patient had gangrene of foot and leg, and I had previously removed his other leg, about two years ago, for the same condition. After complete recovery, he should be able to earn a living on the tea garden, making baskets, etc.

We have arranged to go to Bishnauth to the Christmas party at the club in the evening, and will stay one night with the doctor (Dr Chesshire) and his wife, whom we have not seen for a few months. There are a lot of things I would like to discuss with him before going to the Calcutta office. Dr Gilroy of the Ross Institute had promised to pay a visit before we went on leave, but he had a last-minute call to South India, and will not be able to come over until after our return from home leave.

I have made out the antimalarial programme estimates, week by week, for next year, in accordance with the official Ross Institute recommendations, and hope to have the best results ever recorded in the practice. This was an excellent year on half of the tea gardens, but the other half ran out of insecticide at the height of the transmission period, and spoiled the figures.

Mum

I remember the Christmas parties at Bishnauth. We had the New Year parties at Halem. There would be dancing and "shows", and all the usual entertainment.

14

JANUARY TO JULY 1955

RMS Caledonia, 21st January 1955

Since Christmas, we have hardly had a minute to turn. Reita packed all our belongings into boxes (fourteen of them), and we nailed these down. The Pattullos are storing them for us in a spare room in their bungalow. We flew to Calcutta on 11th January by freight plane, and spent five days catching up with embarkation regulations, banking, etc. I do not know when the ship is due to dock at Liverpool. They do not like to give definite promises, but the reckoning works out about 7th February.

RMS Caledonia

Mum and Dad aboard RMS Caledonia
Eden Rollo (middle): one of the representatives from the British Drug House (whom they met on the "Batory") is seeing them off

Reita will catch the first plane to Islay to see her folks, and after seeing her on board, I will go straight to Dumbarton, which will give me almost two weeks at home, before the course in London starts.

Mum

This would be the last letter before we arrived back in the UK. We arrived in Liverpool. It was pouring with rain, and I had sling-back shoes on. It was very cold. We got the train to Glasgow with our luggage, and went to my sister, Mary's, who said Allan's mother had phoned, asking us both to come to Dumbarton.

I stayed for a couple of weeks, until Allan went to London, and I went to Islay to see my family. Unfortunately, when I arrived in Islay, my father took ill. He was passing blood, and I flew with him to the Southern General in Glasgow, and remained at my sister's (Mary), whilst Allan studied and sat his exams in London.

When Allan was in London, he made contact with us by phone, but sent a note to his mother when he began his exams.

London, 16th July 1955

Just a little note to let you know that I am getting on all right. I sat the two written papers on Wednesday, each of them, three hours: "Parasitology and Bacteriology" in the morning, and "Tropical Hygiene" in the afternoon. I sat another three-hour paper on "Tropical Medicine" on Thursday, and was very glad to get that part of the course completed. On Friday morning, we had a three-hour practical examination in the School (London School of Hygiene and Tropical Medicine). They gave us a stool specimen, a malarial blood film, a section of liver from someone in the Pacific (who had died of a small microscopic liver fluke disease) and ten spot examinations of already prepared microscopic specimens of a variety of tropical conditions.

To-date, I have done quite well. When we were coming out of the School, we met Professor Macdonald, who told us that the practical and clinical examinations (which I will be doing on Monday) are the most important parts of the examination, and that no one can afford to slip up on these. For that reason, John Twomey (we met him on the "Caledonia", and he said he was doing the same course in London) and I have been getting on with our work this weekend as usual, so that we will not make any slips (we hope) on Monday at the Hospital for Tropical Diseases. Professor Macdonald is not an examiner this year, as he had to help out with examinations two weeks ago.

We have no examination on Tuesday, so I will take the opportunity of going over to see George Williamson & Co. On Wednesday, we have oral examinations, but I am not too worried about these. The results come out on Thursday afternoon, and I have already booked a sleeper for the 9.10pm train on Thursday evening (21st July), and will arrive in Dumbarton on Friday.

Reita wants me to go straight over to Islay to spend a short time there, and then she will come back with me. Her father is doing very well, but gets tired at times, and wonders why he has no strength to dress himself. If Reita wants to stay longer with him, I will come back to Dumbarton myself, but I will give you all the news when I see you.

Mum

Fortunately, Allan passed all his exams.

*London School of Hygiene and Tropical Medicine:
DTM&H Course (1955)
Front row: Professor Macdonald (6th from right)
Third row: Dad (5th from right) and John Twomey (6th from right)*

I remember John Twomey very well. He was with his wife and young daughter on the "Caledonia". They were an Irish couple, and were returning from Somalia. Allan and John stayed in the same digs in London. Their landlady was very good to them, and fed them well.

Thinking back, I must have gone back to Dumbarton, because when I first saw Allan, he was wearing winkle pickers, and had a wave in his hair. I made him get rid of the wave, and his mother put the shoes in the bin...

15

SEPTEMBER TO DECEMBER 1955

Mum and Dad were still on leave in Britain in August 1955, so there were no letters for this month. These resumed in September, when they returned to Assam for their second contract.

Dufflaghur Tea Estate, 23rd September 1955

Our flight from Glasgow to London was very pleasant (at 19,000 feet) with breakfast on board. By the time we finished eating and had a smoke, we had almost reached London. The flight from London to Calcutta was also very pleasant, but a bit tiring, as we had to get out at every stop. They fed us very well. By the time we reached Karachi and then Calcutta, the weather was very warm, and what with the lack of sleep and the heat, our appetites disappeared for a couple of days.

    The office car was waiting to take us to our hotel, and when I went into the office on Tuesday, they told me they had booked us for Assam, by air, on the Wednesday. We got some hurried shopping done, and left the hotel the next morning at 6am.

    We were unlucky with our blue case. At the last minute, I forgot to lock it, and when we got to the hotel in Calcutta, we noticed a shoetree was hanging over the side of the case. Stuff had been removed, probably in Beirut where we changed planes. We were lucky with our radio, and only had to pay Rs 88 on it. We have tried it out, and it looks as though it is going to do very well.

On arrival at Tezpur, there was no one to meet us, as the telephone line had been knocked down between Bishnauth and Dufflaghur. Fortunately, the pilot of the tea garden plane had called in to collect a parcel, which had been taken up in the big plane from Calcutta. As he already had one passenger, he was only able to take Reita and half of our luggage up as far as Bishnauth. It was fortuitous that there was a car standing by for a passenger who had not arrived, and I was able to hire it over to a nearby club, where a tea meeting was in progress. So, from Tezpur airport, it took me to Thakurbari club (twelve miles away) and I was able to get lunch and a lift in the small plane, along with some folks returning from the meeting. So, we both finally arrived in Bishnauth, and spent the night with Dr Chesshire and his wife. They are looking forward to their leave, but he will also have to look forward to some hard work in London when his classes start. They have recently had a new son, which makes it one boy and one girl.

We arrived in Dufflaghur the next day (Thursday), and have now settled back into the bungalow. Since our arrival, there has been no rain, and it has been very warm, especially in bed at night. At the present moment I am struggling with only a pair of shorts, and the fan going full out. In ten minutes, we will have our first Assam curry from our new cook (obtained by the locum doctor, who took over when we were on leave). I suppose we will settle down within a week or two, when we get back to our usual activities again.

I hope you are feeling fine, and not staying up too late to watch the TV!

Mum

When we left Liverpool for Glasgow by train, we kept seeing these funny metal things on the chimneys, and couldn't think what they were. It was only later we found out they were aerials for televisions. Allan bought his mother the TV he refers to, for her birthday. It had a very small screen, and only showed BBC1 in black and white. It was the first time we had ever watched television, and Allan's father liked to watch the "News" and the "Boxing".

Dufflaghur Tea Estate, 2nd October 1955

We are now back to our usual again, but felt tired and lazy for about five days or so after our arrival, due to the sudden change and the heat. The planters were saying that this was the hottest spell of weather they had had during the year.

Our wireless is still doing very well, but we do not know all the wavelengths for the BBC in this part of the world. Could you find out the address of the BBC in London for me, and I will write to them for full particulars of their short-wave broadcasts? I am glad the two of you are enjoying the TV. It would be grand if we could have one out here, but the chances of that are very remote indeed; although possibly, Calcutta will have TV in a year or so.

We went to the club (Halem) for the first time on Thursday evening, and got a good reception from everyone. Reita is busy getting the bungalow in order just now, and ordering up stores from Calcutta. We have planted some beans and also some cabbages and cauliflowers. It is too early, however, to go ahead with everything. After 15th October is reckoned to be safe from the deluge point of view. We should get our flowers into the ground by the beginning of November, including delphiniums.

Dufflaghur Tea Estate, 10th October 1955

We were very pleased to receive your letter and hear that you are doing fine. I am sure the boxing match must have been very good on TV. We are getting good reception with our new radio. Our old one was out of commission by the time we got back – resistances burned out, I presume.

No sooner had I arrived back on the tea garden, when I got a letter from Calcutta asking for a report on all the hospitals, in view of the new Act passed by the Government of India, defining the tea garden hospital standards.

Mum

That was Allan back to hard work again – nose to the grindstone...

Dufflaghur Tea Estate, 17th October 1955

We have now settled in. Reita is rearranging her curtains, and arranging for pelmets. After that, we will get a bit of painting done to freshen the house up.

It has been very wet since Wednesday of last week. All the roads have been flooded, and the Boroi River is uncrossable. It will be another month before the cold weather bridge over the Boroi goes up. Until then, I will have to keep on wading. Still, it keeps my feet clean??!!

This year has been a very good one from the health point of view. The malaria control programme, in particular, has gone very nicely, and this gives me quite a bit of satisfaction, after the amount of work I put into it, before we left.

The Pattullos are doing well. Pat is only going to do one more year, and then he is going home for good. He will be retiring before his time, but feels he cannot carry on any longer than that.

Mum

When they did eventually leave, I really missed them. I even missed their dog!

Dufflaghur Tea Estate, 26th October 1955

On Sunday, we went over to Bishnauth to see their new 35mm cinema in action. The projector is the same size as the one in the cinemas at home. I had had an urgent call, in the morning, to the other side of the river, and the acting manager had asked us to come back and stay the night, so we could see the film.

On the Monday night, we stayed with Dr Chesshire, as I had business to talk over with him, and we did not get back to our own bungalow until midday on Tuesday. It was, however, a very pleasant change. The last three days have been religious festivals for Hindus, but things have quietened down again.

Mum

There were always festivals, and the drums would be going all night. The men would drink their "Sulai pheni", and there would be a few sore heads in the morning.

Puja Drums

Dufflaghur Tea Estate, 3rd November 1955

We are getting on fine, anxiously awaiting the arrival of our stuff (travelling by sea on the "City of Chester"), hoping it will be intact. I got a letter from Michael (a German doctor on the London course). He has been in London until recently, and has now almost completed his arrangements to go to Nigeria at the end of December. He was saying that eleven people failed the examination. I have not yet written to John Twomey, who is now back in Somaliland, but will do so in the next few days.

This is our club night, however, as there is no film tonight, we have decided to stay at home. I often go for tennis in the afternoon, when there is no film at night, but as my sandals have not yet arrived, I will have to leave it.

The planters say that there was quite a serious drought at the beginning of this year, and many of the tea bushes died. Our good old lemon tree has survived, however, and so have the other two jungly ones we planted, but I will have to yank them out.

Mum

Sandals? What did he want sandals for? It was plimsolls you were supposed to wear to play tennis. Anyway, I was waiting for a cotton skirt to wear at the New Year pantomime. We were going to be performing American Square Dancing. Allan was doing it as well – and I can tell you now, he wouldn't be wearing sandals for that either!

Dufflaghur Tea Estate, 14th November 1955

We read in the newspaper that the "City of Chester" arrived in Calcutta on 5th November. We have not yet heard about our baggage, and are hoping it will be all right. I have been very busy this week as Dr Chesshire is on leave, and I have had to go over to see some urgent cases in his district. The temporary bridge over the Boroi River, however, is almost ready, and that should make a big difference.

The weather is now very pleasant here. This week is a festival for Hindus, and they are celebrating hard. Most of the labourers get very drunk, and the servants are all getting off to perform in the festivities.

Puja Festival

The vegetables are beginning to look well in the back garden. We had our first beans about ten days ago. After the festival, we will get all our flowers planted.

Mum

Sulai pheni...

Dufflaghur Tea Estate, 25th November 1955

The weather out here is just lovely now, but Reita feels the cold at night as we have not received our baggage yet, and the hot water bottle bag is among our stuff. Because our baggage is in Calcutta, I have filled in a custom's declaration form, and sent it to the agents. It is doubtful, however, whether we will receive it before Christmas, and we will be left without dress clothes for the parties at that time.

Our jungle road is not open yet. The temporary Boroi Bridge, which promised to be ready so quickly this year, will be ready by tomorrow or Monday. I have been walking over the bridge on foot for the last fortnight. Our garden is looking very well. We have been eating beans and radishes from it. Reita still has a lot to do, however, to get it as she wants it.

Verna has started canvassing the "Football Pools" in Assam. They send the Pool in advance, and it is returned by airmail. I am half thinking of starting to fill it in, as I could do with the extra £75,000!! The manager of Halem Tea Estate came back from leave on the "Caledonia" and said that the deck steward got a wire from his wife, on arrival in Bombay, stating they had won £75,000. He immediately took the next plane for home!

The rice all around us is getting ripe. It is just like a field of wheat. After another week, they will be very busy getting it harvested.

Our wireless and new clock are working well. The "eight-day" clock is most useful as it keeps good time and allows us to check up on all the others. I wrote, this evening, to the "Voices of America" to get their frequencies and relay stations, so that we can try a change of listening from time to time.

Mum

I don't know who the deck steward was, but £75,000 was a great deal of money in those days. I don't even remember Allan "doing the Pools" in Assam. But when we got back to the UK, although he wasn't interested in football itself, he was an ardent supporter of "The Pools". I suppose it was the equivalent of the lottery. I don't think he ever won anything. I do remember, however, one Saturday night, watching the results for him, whilst he was working at the surgery. I thought we'd won, but I got things back to front, and we hadn't won anything. He was most disappointed.

Dufflaghur Tea Estate, 5th December 1955

We went to Tezpur on Saturday to do some shopping, and had a puncture about ten miles out of the town, and another slow one, in the town itself. On our way back, we had another two punctures, and had to borrow a repair outfit from one of the assistants, who was passing (by good fortune), as our own one, by that time, was out of commission. We might have been isolated all night, but eventually got home about 10pm. To crown it all, the sandwiches we took with us must have been bad, as we were both sick after our return. However, all is well now.

I had a letter from Dr Gilroy of the Ross Institute, some time ago. He is away to Geneva, and will later go on to the Sudan, returning to Assam about February or March. Mrs Gilroy had an operation about six weeks ago, and will have a holiday in the South of France, while Dr Gilroy is attending to his WHO (World Health Organisation) business.

No baggage yet. Both radios are fixed up – the big one in our sitting room, and the small set in the bedroom.

Mum

I don't remember that particular incident with the punctures, but we were always having problems on the road. There was always something happening to the Land Rover. If it wasn't the Land Rover, it was the road, which was nothing more than a dirt track. Many a night we were stranded till the morning.

Dufflaghur Tea Estate, 18th December 1955

I had a mild attack of dysentery, this week. It started on Tuesday, and lasted until yesterday, despite all the drugs I was consuming. I had one day in bed, but have not done very much this week. Reita has kept completely free of infection. The preparations for Christmas have now started. We are going to a party at the Bishnauth Club, and will stay one night with the Chesshires. At our own club, we will be giving a party on Hogmanay, with an amateur theatrical "show" at the same time. We have still not received our luggage, and are shivering every night, as the evenings have become very cold, and the quality of the coal this year, is very poor.

We have been having cook trouble for some weeks. The present one is due to leave at the end of the month. Reita will be cooking until we get another one, but it should not be too difficult in the cold weather, compared to her last "bout" in the middle of the monsoon. Cooking with primitive facilities, however, is always rather difficult.

We went to a wedding on Thursday. One of the planters brought his daughter out to Assam at the beginning of the year, and she has married one of the assistant managers.

Mum

No cook! Waiting on baggage! Allan's sandals – or, should I say, plimsolls! My skirt! It was just as well Allan didn't have a gun! But I remember the wedding well. They were a lovely couple. Joy (the bride) later had two boys (Rupert and Nigel) very near to each other. At Christmas, I bought them a drum each, and they were very noisy.

Dufflaghur Tea Estate, 30th December 1955

Our baggage arrived, by air, on Saturday, and we collected it from the airfield (about thirty miles away) on Sunday afternoon. We had to force the lock of the big trunk. We had left the keys in Calcutta, but they were not returned. Customs had taken everything out for examination, and the travel agents had repacked it. After checking the contents (everything was there), we had to get our stuff pressed for the party at Bishnauth. We got there very late, but enjoyed ourselves.

Since then, I have been waiting for the keys, but they have not arrived, so we burst the padlock securing the tin trunk, and Reita will go through the stuff tonight. Everything appears to be in good order (even the dishes), despite damage to one corner of the outside of this trunk.

Tomorrow will be our "show" at the club. The young fellows have been working very hard, and have produced a sort of pantomime, lasting half an hour, which should amuse everyone. The "wind", "lightning" and "thunder" effects, at one part, are marvellous. The patter is also excellent, involving a "skit" at everything possible concerning tea. There is a mannequin parade of men dressed up — again, excellent dialogue.

Since the cook left, the other servants have all had a bash at it, and the cooking has been simple, but lovely. Everything given out, has gone into it, and the fat has been changed regularly. Fats can be dangerous out here, due to imperceptible sprue. I am now wondering if I had the cook to thank for my dysentery infection.

Mum

At last! The baggage! The pantomime went very well at New Year. We did our American Square Dancing — including Allan with his two left feet. I got my hot water bottle and skirt. I made arrangements for the cooking. I don't remember too much about the "sandals", but I certainly didn't find a gun…

16

JANUARY TO DECEMBER 1956

Dufflaghur Tea Estate, 8th January 1956

We are both in good health, and have settled into our usual way again after Christmas and New Year festivities. We went up the jungle river for a picnic today. It was a great tonic to get into the open air, swimming, etc.

Dad swimming in the River Boroi

A wild elephant crossed the river, about one hundred yards downstream from the picnic area. It was a glorious sight, and not one that we get the chance to see very often.

I am in the middle of the annual musters just now. I have examined about ten thousand people to-date – eyes of adults and spleens of children.

Annual Muster

Mum

I remember the elephant. It really was a picturesque sight. It was on the other side of the river on its own, and came marching clumsily through the water in our direction. It simply ignored us, and leaving the river, climbed up rocks and disappeared.

Allan did quite a number of musters, and would have to leave early in the morning in warm clothes because it was cold. For the annual ones, he had to go round all the tea gardens, and examine the labour forces and their children before they started their work.

Dufflaghur Tea Estate, 22nd January 1956

We have had a busy week. An urgent call arrived at 2.30am on Thursday morning to go out to one of the tea gardens about eighteen miles from here, to attend the wife of one of the assistant managers (European). She was in labour by the time I arrived (seven months of pregnancy), and it was not until 11.25am that we got the delivery completed, and produced a baby girl of 3lbs 5½oz. The child was badly asphyxiated at birth, and hardly able to breathe owing to prematurity. I had to work on her for almost an hour, before we got respiration firmly established, and her colour changed from blue to a nice pink.

After that, we got cylinders of oxygen from one of the neighbouring tea gardens to have in readiness, should the respiration again become laboured. It was fortunate we did, for the baby developed another attack of feeble respiration, lasting three-quarters of an hour in the evening, and the oxygen was literally life-saving.

On Friday morning, we took the mother and baby to the mission hospital in Tezpur, by car, giving oxygen all the way. The baby took the journey very well, and it looks as if everything might be all right. This was the first time Reita has attended a confinement, and she was quite pleased to get the opportunity. Yesterday and today, we have been making up as much sleep as possible. The record for my practice is 2lbs 1½ oz. This was an Indian baby. The average weight at birth on a tea garden is about 5lbs. Unfortunately, for every one we save, we lose quite a number of the very small ones, especially as so much depends on the knowledge of the mother.

The weather has been very cold, with grey skies and rain, during the last few days. I think so far it is the coldest cold weather we have had. The vegetables are now ready, except for the tomatoes, which will take another fortnight. Reita planted the delphinium seeds in the back garden, but nothing appeared, and we do not see them advertised in "Sutton's Calcutta" booklet. I think this part of the world must be unsuitable for them. We have a good array of rose cuttings coming up in boxes, but we will wait for a while before planting them out. There is no word about a locum for Dr Chesshire yet. I will probably have to take over both practices. He leaves in the middle of February.

Dufflaghur Tea Estate, 5th February 1956

There is a "do" at the neighbouring club today – tennis, during the day, and supper and dancing, in the evening. We will go over tonight, as we are not tennis enthusiasts. The Company has managed to obtain a locum for Dr Chesshire during his leave. He leaves, by air, about 15th February, and will be taking the course at the London School of Hygiene and Tropical Medicine. We will probably see them tonight. The locum is an Indian gentleman, who qualified in Edinburgh, and is now retired. He does tea garden work to keep himself amused.

Dufflaghur Tea Estate, 21st February 1956

Our weather has been very pleasant, and Reita took her first plunge in the jungle river on Sunday. After she got in, we could not get her to come out. The water was just lovely. It is her birthday today. She says she is twenty-one again!

The sickness rates at the hospitals are at their lowest just now. There have been a few cases of pneumonia in adults and children, however, and a lot of cuts and injuries due to the pruning and clearing up.

Dr Chesshire will be in the UK now. He starts the course in London on 27th February. Both he and his wife are graduates of Durham University. I am not sure where they come from, but it probably will not be very far away.

Unfortunately, the baby I delivered died at Tezpur hospital, despite all efforts to keep her alive. She had gone down to 2lbs 8oz from 3lbs 5½oz, in three weeks.

Our back garden is at its peak just now. We have lovely peas, cabbages, cauliflowers and tomatoes. All are grown outside. We also have some strawberries, which managed to stay alive in the hot weather, and then blossomed forth during the cold weather.

Mum

We were very sad when the baby died. The parents (Caroline and Roy Eastment) were heart-broken. Everyone had striven so hard to keep her alive. Fortunately, Caroline had another baby girl (Diana), a couple of years later, and I was godmother to her.

Mum and Dad with Diana

Dufflaghur Tea Estate, 9th March 1956

We were pleased to receive two letters, and hope that you are all in good health. Thank you for the General Medical Council form, which I will fill in and return to them in order to have my name retained on the medical register.

Reita and I went to a "show" in one of the clubs, about one hundred and twenty miles along the bank, last weekend. On the way there, I went into the Halem post office to ask the postmaster to put a letter into the Halem mailbag. As the post office was closed, I went to his house at the back. While speaking to him, a dog (from the

Halem line) kept running around and barking. The next thing I knew, it had stuck its teeth into the calf of my leg. Fortunately, I know this dog, otherwise I would have been thinking of rabies. I still gave my wound a good scrub. I saw the dog today, and will see it again on Monday. If it is all right, then my conscience will be completely clear.

A dog suffering from rabies cannot live for more than a week, but we always take ten days for safety. The children of one of the assistants at Halem were bitten by a three-month old puppy from the line, a couple of weeks ago. As the dog died less than a week later, it was necessary to give antirabic injections, despite the fact the dog (apparently) died of natural causes and not hydrophobia.

Last week, one of the old planters retired. He got an urgent call, as he would have been taxed for another year at the resident rate, if he had not left India before the end of the month! The Pattullos are retiring in one year from now. They feel they cannot get away quickly enough. We had dinner with them on Saturday, and saw some lovely coloured films. I must send for some coloured spools – the results are just lovely.

Mum

I didn't see the dog actually bite Allan. I was sitting waiting for him in the Land Rover, and he was an awful long time coming back. I didn't hear or see the pye-dog, but when Allan returned to the vehicle, he was in a terrible state. We couldn't get home quickly enough. He used soap, water and a scrubbing brush to clean the wound. He scrubbed so hard, it left a permanent scar.

Fortunately, he was fine. We still went to the "show" that evening, but we never really settled until we were certain the dog didn't have rabies.

Dufflaghur Tea Estate, 22nd March 1956

Thank you for your two letters. We were amused to hear about the Dufflas on TV. Shortly after we arrived back in Assam, our Duffla pal rolled up to the bungalow one day, looking for the lighter, fishing rod and knife that I had, apparently, promised to bring back from

"Beelat" for him. We gave him an old lighter, and had to make excuses about the other items. "Beelat" is the name for the UK, derived from "Blighty", as used by the British Army in India.

The dog, which bit me a few weeks ago, is still alive and doing well, so I do not need to worry about developing rabies. It has never bitten anyone before, or since that time. The animals out here get quite agitated when a light-skinned person comes near them, as they are not accustomed to this. The small children sometimes get frightened also.

The last six months appear to have flown past. The bamboo bridge is still there, but they have started preparations for a permanent steel bridge across the Boroi River. This will take some time to complete – probably about eighteen months.

The mosquitoes are now making their appearance, and the anti-malarial programme is underway. The results, last year, were satisfactory, and we are hoping to improve them even more this year.

Mum

I remember the Duffla, but I don't remember Allan promising to bring him anything back from the UK. I think it would have been down to miscommunication. Fortunately, we were able to give him something, although I don't know how he refilled the lighter, because he never came back.

Dufflaghur Tea Estate, 1st April 1956

Today, we went up the jungle river for our usual picnic. We were the only Europeans there, and found that a gang of Dufflas had set up camp nearby. They came over to see us, and see what we would give them. In the end, we gave them the ice cubes from our thermos flask, and they passed them around to each other, highly delighted. When the monsoon comes, they will disappear into their villages in the hills until next year. One of them was a good speaker of the tea garden language, and told us his village was three days' journey into the hills, and that they had a population of more than three hundred. I do wonder, however, if they have ever counted the population.

Mum

I remember the incident with the ice cubes. They were highly amused, and kept popping them in their mouths. The funny thing was, we never ever saw a Duffla woman.

Dufflaghur Tea Estate, 21st April 1956

We were pleased to receive your letters, and interested to hear about Professor Macdonald on TV. He is on the up-and-up, and will probably take over from Professor Macintosh when he retires. This would make him the number one authority on public health matters in Britain. Professor Macdonald has a wide experience in tropical matters, as well as health in temperate climates.

We heard the Scotland v England match last Saturday. It was very exciting. We have just heard the result of the Hearts v Celtic match straight from Scotland on thirteen metres. We also get good reception straight from London on eleven metres. London reception, at the moment, is better than Ceylon, Singapore (also BBC) and Australia.

I have ordered a record player from Calcutta so that we can always be sure of getting good reception, even during the monsoon thunder and lightning. We will play records through the radio. Some of the managers have a good set-up for record playing, and we are ordering the same type as one of theirs, so that there will be no difficulty with our Murphy set. It is very powerful, and the modern long-playing records are just grand.

Tomorrow (Sunday) we will have a picnic and swim. Our Duffla pals have disappeared again, which is a blessing, as the aroma of their presence is not always "eau de cologne". They are rather allergic to water for other than drinking purposes...

We have been listening with great interest, to the visit of the Russian leaders to Britain. Let us hope that some true reduction of tension will result. This exposure of Stalin's activities reminds me of the feeling I had when Hess landed in Scotland.

Mum

I loved the record player. I used to play the "Bluebell Polka", and dance away by myself.

Dufflaghur Tea Estate, 20th May 1956

The bamboo bridge over the Boroi River has been washed away, so we are now into hot weather isolation. Our cold storage is still coming up from Calcutta by air, direct to the tea garden about twenty-five miles away. Unfortunately, on Tuesday, when it should have arrived, because of the weather, the freight plane only got as far as Gauhati where they have radio-controlled landing arrangements. It turned back to Calcutta and came up again on Thursday when the weather improved – but the condition of the beef had not improved, and we had to throw it out. I hope this kind of thing does not happen too often, or we will have to go back to the old goat again – and that is not a pleasant thought. Our vegetables are now almost finished. We only have onions, carrots, etc, left, and not many of those. We will be on to the indigenous stuff in another two or three weeks. We had a terrific crop this year – it is the only way we can be sure of getting enough for ourselves.

I have bought a few rolls of colour film, and am going to try them out when the weather improves. I cannot take any chances with it, as the slightest error will waste the film.

Mum

I remember the beef being bad when it arrived, and we had to throw it out. I'm not sure how we sourced the beef, since cows were considered holy in India.

Dufflaghur Tea Estate, 4th June 1956

We have just received bad news from Islay, to say that Reita's father had died. He took pleurisy near the beginning of May, and was transferred to the local hospital. Sadly, despite treatment, he was not able to gather strength, and died on 21st May at 8.30am. This has been a great shock for Reita, who was expecting him to rally, as he has always done in the past. She felt she would see him again before he died, but this was not to be. The gravestone, which he had ordered for Reita's mother, had already arrived in Islay, but he did not get a chance to see it.

Mum's mother

There was a big turnout of men at his funeral. He was well known to everyone in the village.

Mum

At that time, it was usually the men who went to funerals; and as Allan says, my father, whom we called "Rop", was well known in Bowmore. He'd been a fisherman.

"Rop" showing off a newly-caught fish!

Dufflaghur Tea Estate, 25th June 1956

I have been very busy for the last fortnight, writing reports on tea garden facilities. Delays at the Boroi River are a constant annoyance, which is increased when there is a lot of work to do. However, there is no use grumbling.

The gramophone and some records have arrived from Calcutta. They came up on the freight plane without any trouble, and the records are playing very nicely through the radio. Reita will get a lot of fun from it.

At the present moment, the "mistris" (tradesmen) are scraping the walls of the bungalow in preparation for redecoration. This is the first touch of paint and waterproof distemper in five years; however, the bungalow should be very nice afterwards, and that raises Reita's morale enormously.

The Naga tribesmen still appear to be giving some trouble, but the trouble spots are very far from this side of the river.

Mum

I can't remember much about the Nagas, except they lived in the Naga Hills, and I believe the issue was maybe to do with independence.

Dufflaghur Tea Estate, 14th July 1956

The weather has been very warm with the fans going full blast. Fungi are growing over the books and papers. The only contact we have with the outside world just now, is through the radio and newspapers. Reita, however, is getting fed up with the wireless, as every time we turn it on, we can hear nothing but cricket. The sound is so good, it is as if the match were only a couple of miles away, instead of a few thousand miles away. The results come through the BBC, All India Radio, Radio Ceylon and Australia. Everybody seems to be listening in.

We have not heard from Arthur Chesshire since he went on leave. He will be getting ready for his examinations in a week or two. I have met the locum only a few times, and he seems quite a nice fellow. On Monday, he wants me to take out a tooth for his wife. She had the tooth filled, but it has apparently turned septic.

We are going to a "show" at the Bishnauth Club on Saturday, and will be staying on the other side of the river until Monday. This should be a nice change, as we have hardly left the bungalow for ages, and this "hermit" type of existence is very bad for one's psychological outlook in life.

We had a little earthquake a few nights ago, but it only lasted for a couple of minutes. The bungalow swayed gently, the roof creaked, and then the whole thing was over. Some of the sparrows which had nested under the eaves, however, got a fright and flew out of the nest in the dark. One of them landed on the wire mesh at the door, and looked a bit startled.

Mum

No wonder! We were all feeling a bit startled! I believe the locum he refers to was Dr Chopra. He and his family were very nice. I think Allan must have got a reputation for taking out teeth. We certainly didn't need a dentist, nor did we need a vet. He used to treat pets as well, and he never charged for his dental or veterinary services.

Dufflaghur Tea Estate, 24th July 1956

We are still in the middle of decorating. They have not yet completed half of the bungalow, so we are still in turmoil and sleeping in the spare bedroom at present.

We have been having very heavy rain for the last few days, and all the roads are flooded. The mail and cold storage did not get across the Boroi River today, but we hope they will get over tomorrow, otherwise the cold storage will be a dead loss.

We went to the "show" at Bishnauth Club on Saturday. They put on the usual amateur cabaret for twenty minutes, with wisecracks about everyone worked into the patter. It was very good and very cleverly worked out.

Mr Lunsdaine from the Calcutta office was there. He had flown up on the previous Thursday. He also paid us a visit on Monday, to discuss hospital records. They want to eliminate some of the statistical reduplication, and would like to try out a new system here, to see whether it will work, and what modifications may be required. I do not know if I am pleased or not, as this will no doubt involve me in extra work, and at times I have felt extra work is expected of me.

Reita is doing fine. She is fiddling about with curtains at the moment. Some day she will get them exactly as she wants them!!! The record player and radio are doing fine. We have a long player of Scottish country dances, and Reita gives me a demonstration every now and then. It is so funny to see her galloping across the floor on her own, practising each dance.

Mum

Galloping? Galloping? Really! I thought I was very dainty!

Dufflaghur Tea Estate, 14th August 1956

The house decorating is still going on slowly, and we will be glad to see it finished.

The tea gardens have all been helping with the erection of a new club building at Halem. The old one was getting very dilapidated. The new one is now almost finished, and is looking very nice. The opening ceremony is to be held on 1st September. It is to be a weekend "show". People from the other side of the river will be put up in bungalows on this side, for two days. There will be Saturday night dancing and cabaret – and on Sunday night, a film.

I am hoping that Dr Gilroy of the Ross Institute will manage to come over to pay a visit to the practice, next month. It is a long time since he has been, and I have a lot of problems I would like to put to him.

Dufflaghur Tea Estate, 9th September 1956

Happy Birthday, Mother! I cannot remember if you are forty-two or sixty-two! We had the opening celebrations at the new club last weekend. There were a lot of visitors (from outside) staying in this district. Unfortunately, I had urgent calls both days, and missed a considerable part of it.

Reita went to Shillong yesterday, for a little holiday. The manager and his wife (Guy and Peggy Heefke from Halem) were going up in their Land Rover on company business, and asked her if she would like to take the opportunity of having a little change from the heat of the plains. I am expecting them back on Friday. In the meantime, I will get on with the clerical work, which keeps piling up.

We are hoping to take local leave (in November) at one of the popular seaside resorts in Orissa, which is about two hundred miles south of Calcutta. We thought of Darjeeling, but it would be very cold in November, and the houses in India are not made for warmth.

One of the Scottish managers was murdered on the south bank, about a week ago. The labour force had been making threats for some time, and there had been a great deal of dispute on his tea garden. It was a great shock to everyone. His wife had a cousin in Falkirk, who was a patient of mine. It appears that they stabbed him repeatedly, and almost severed his head. When his wife went out into the tea garden to see what was happening, they told her that they had all taken part in it. His dog was sitting beside his body.

It is very difficult to pass judgement on this type of thing, but certainly, murder is not a twentieth century way of settling any grievance. The police have taken away about seven or eight of the ringleaders.

An Indian manager on a nearby tea garden, was also murdered only a few months ago, and even the labour union is up in arms about it.

Mum

These murders took place on the south bank of the Brahmaputra. We were on the north bank, so I didn't know too much about them, except that the Scottish manager was more or less cut up into pieces. It was horrible.

Dufflaghur Tea Estate, 24th September 1956

Reita had a nice holiday in Shillong, and got some shopping done. We are looking forward to our local leave, and have decided to go to Gopalpur, which is on the coast, south of Calcutta. This part of the country will be completely new to us, including the language, but I do not expect too much language trouble. We are expecting to see some of the old Hindu temples and have some bathing in the sea. It will still be warm there in November, when Assam has turned cold.

On our way back, we will stay for a few days in Calcutta. It will be quite nice to see a big town again, after one year of isolation.

The decorators have made a lovely job of the bungalow, but have run out of paint. They will have to do the spare bedroom in the cold weather.

Dr Gilroy of the Ross Institute is coming over a week today, to help out with a malaria problem in one of the tea gardens. He will be staying for a few days, and we are looking forward to his visit.

Thank you for sending the record catalogue. Our record player is working very nicely, and we have a good selection of records. The wireless reception from London is excellent just now, but the "News", particularly Suez (*Suez Crisis*), is a bit depressing.

Dufflaghur Tea Estate, 10th October 1956

We had Dr Gilroy of the Ross Institute staying with us from Monday to Thursday, last week. He was helping with a malaria problem on one of the tea gardens, and took a look round most of the other tea gardens during his stay. He was most interesting – also most helpful. (He was in the Sudan for six months last year, on behalf of WHO, to advise on malaria problems.)

We have arranged to go to Gopalpur (in Orissa) between 13th and 19th November, with a few days in Calcutta on our way back. It will be quite a change to see tarred roads again. In Gopalpur, we will be staying at the Palm Beach Hotel. We had a conjurer at the club (Halem) last week. He was doing an off-season tour of Calcutta, Delhi, etc, and the agency houses hired him to do a quick tour of the Assam clubs. His name is George Brand, and he told us they had stopped him doing TV because he had had a few too many to drink, and made some vulgar remarks. Some of the stories he told us would not have met the television standards! However, he was very clever and entertaining. He pushed a lighted cigarette through the club bearer's coat, and the look of amazement on his face was very amusing when no mark could be found on the man's coat afterwards.

Mum

Just as well! He wanted to do the same trick with my dress – only I told him where to go...

Gopalpur, 16th November 1956

We left the tea garden, by plane, on Saturday, and had a difficult time in finding suitable accommodation in Calcutta because we had no prior booking. Fortunately, the manager of Halem and his wife (Guy and Peggy Heefke) were on the same plane, and they took us to the club in Calcutta, where we got a good meal after our journey. After two days in Calcutta, we travelled by night train to Gopalpur, arriving here on Tuesday at 6am. Since then, we have been bathing in the Indian Ocean regularly, three times daily.

My appetite has increased one hundred percent or more, and my muscles are just beginning to recover from the first aches of unaccustomed exercise.

Our room looks out on to the sand, and the sun is very strong. At night, however, the temperature is quite comfortable. We are sleeping with only a sheet – no blankets. It will be a big change to go back to Assam, where fires will be required every night by now. The distance from Assam must be about the same as the South of France from Glasgow. The main industry is fishing, and the local people draw in good catches in their nets at this time of year. Every type of fish is available on the hotel menu – and what a change from the fresh water fish in Assam.

We leave for Calcutta on Monday evening, and will have five days there before flying up to Assam on 25th November. A booking has already been made at a boarding house, so we will have no worry about our accommodation, and will probably go to the pictures every night.

Mum

In Gopalpur, we were never out the water. The waves were high, and an Indian boy escorted each European to stop them drowning. I was lucky – I had two!

Left to right: Mum, Dad and Peggy

I don't know why he said it was a boarding house in Calcutta. We stayed at the Grand Hotel! And we went to Princes Night Club, which was attached to it.

Mum and Dad dancing at Princes Night Club

One evening, someone was selling red roses, and Allan bought me one. The next time he bought me flowers was out of Morrison's supermarket, forty odd years later – and that was only because they were half price...

I recall going to the pictures in Calcutta, and the film I remember seeing was "Rock around the Clock". All the Indian teenagers were dancing up and down the aisles, enjoying themselves.

Dufflaghur Tea Estate, 1st December 1956

We arrived back at the tea garden last Sunday, and are gradually getting settled into our usual routine. The holiday was very enjoyable.

The world situation seems to be a little easier. No doubt there will be plenty of squabbling before the various problems are settled.

We have heard that Dr Chesshire is coming back in February. When he returns, he is being transferred to a practice on the south bank, and his locum, Dr Chopra, will be carrying on in Bishnauth. Dr Chopra is an Indian doctor, who qualified in the UK, and is a very nice chap. He retired from the Railways a few years ago, and has been doing jobs in Tea.

The south bank practice, where Dr Chesshire is going, is quite near one of the general hospitals in Tea, so facilities for diagnosis and further study will be good. The last doctor there, however, only stayed his three years, and then departed. This was about a month ago.

The Pattullos are on local leave in Shillong at the moment. They are off for good in March. Fortunately, before the Suez crisis, they had arranged to go via South Africa for a holiday on their way home.

Mum

We were on the north bank – the jungly part. The facilities on the south bank were much better, and Allan continually strove to improve the standards of the north side. It turned out he was banging his head against a brick wall.

Dufflaghur Tea Estate, 24th December 1956

Tomorrow, we are going down to Bishnauth for their Christmas party in the evening, and will stay the night with the girl (Caroline) who had the premature baby that died when she was in my practice. She and her husband will stay the night with us for the Hogmanay party here.

Reita decided to have a dog, about three weeks ago – or, should I say, she was talked into it by Caroline! It was a nice Labrador pup, and only three months old. Unfortunately, when it started on the carpets, curtains, etc, with its teeth, Reita nearly had a fit! The little pools of water increased in number in direct proportion to the excitement of the moment. It had a bite at every bush in the back garden, loved knocking over cabbages, and took great pleasure in scattering the rose petals in one bite. It loved shoes – and especially, bare toes. The crowning blow was when it put both legs around Reita's ankles in order to get a more effective bite at her! From what I've said, you can gather that we only kept him for two weeks – yet despite his tricks, I was quite sorry to see him go. On a more practical level, it is not really good policy to keep dogs, as one never knows when it will be bitten by a mad jackal, or taken away by a leopard. The latter fate is the usual finale with dogs out here.

Dad and the pup

We have a small colony of rats on the roof of the bungalow just now. They have been driven in because the rice has now been cut and cleared away. For the past few days, they have been raiding the storeroom and chewing things up. This is the climbing black rat, which is different from the burrowing brown rat, seen at home. As soon as we get the storeroom sealed up, they will probably disappear.

To finish the subject of rats, I now hear of an outbreak of plague at Gauhati, which is on the south bank, about two hundred miles away; no doubt, infected rats carried up on the river steamers with the grain cargoes from Calcutta.

We have decided to go to the BMA meeting in Panitola, next year. We are going to fly up from Tezpur. After the meeting, we will return with Dr and Mrs Gilroy, by car, spend a night at Jorhat, and then fly back to Tezpur. This will, no doubt, be our last BMA meeting in Assam.

Thank you for the calendar, which arrived tonight. Reita joins me in sending our best wishes for Christmas and the New Year.

17

JANUARY TO DECEMBER 1957

Dufflaghur Tea Estate, 7th January 1957

The weather is very pleasant, and the evenings definitely cold. Reita's hot water bag burst a couple of weeks ago, and we had to send a wire to Calcutta for a new one. I was glad to see it arrive, as the noise of her teeth knocking together made it difficult for me to sleep??!!

Our New Year party at the club (Halem) went off very nicely. Ina Pattullo and Reita did the stew for eighty people. The poor old cook was working double time on the previous two days to get things ready, and Reita spent more time in the cookhouse than in the bungalow.

The cook gave us a present of a fish and fowl the other day, as it was the naming ceremony of his new son, delivered by me in a great hurry, a few months ago. I remember getting cross with the old midwife, and chasing her out of the room. Her ideas of obstetrics would have filled a book on "what not to do".

I got a call to see the cook's cow (first baby!) in obstetrical difficulties, on Saturday. With a little help, however, she soon completed the job. I'll have to pull the cook's leg, and ask him what he is going to give me for that job!

The weather is very cold today, due to rain and a dull sky. The back garden will benefit, nevertheless. The delphinium seeds are now coming up nicely. The plants are still very small, but look healthy. Reita spends quite a bit of time in the garden, and enjoys it fine.

The Pattullos are due off in about six weeks. We will be sorry to see them go.

Mum

I remember the two days in the cookhouse getting the stew sorted. Fortunately, since it was January, the heat wouldn't have been too bad. The stew would have been made with all the vegetables from the back garden and cooked over a coal fire.

Dufflaghur Tea Estate, 29th January 1957

Reita has been working in the garden a lot, recently. The delphiniums are growing this year. However, compared to the dahlias, they are very slow. She put them in a box in the relative shade at first, and then transplanted them into the open, and is wondering if this was the right thing to do.

Unfortunately, we have larvae attacking the peas this year, and have lost a lot of plants, just when they were about to produce peas for us. However, our second lot seems to be coming on quite well. The tomatoes will be ready for eating in ten days' time, and the cabbages and cauliflowers have been huge this year.

We had the ICI (Imperial Chemical Industries) man staying with us for a night during his tour of Assam, and he advised about the peas; unfortunately, despite BHC spraying, the first lot has been very poor.

Dr Gilroy is going to publish the district's malaria control figures this year. The 1956 figures have now been made up, and are the best ever recorded. On Dufflaghur, the sick rate from all causes had decreased by 40% from that of five years ago, as the result of efficient malaria control.

I have just received a 10ml vial of the latest antirabic vaccine for dogs (from Lederle in New York) through the BMA (Assam Branch). When the vial is opened, the injections must all be completed in an hour. We are going to have some fun with howling, frightened, fighting, big and small dogs, next week!

Mum

I remember the dogs getting their injections. Because Allan only had an hour, they were brought to the bungalow, where they were all very good. None of them bit him, and they seemed to take the experience in their stride. His animal skills were obviously coming up to par with his human ones!

Dufflaghur Tea Estate, 13th February 1957

I do not know when I will be able to post this letter, as the post office staffs in Assam have gone on strike for a dearness allowance, to compensate for the high cost of living in Assam. I expect it will get dispatched very soon, and that they will get their allowance, as they are at present grossly underpaid. The local postmaster has the rank of assistant postmaster because the post offices are so small, and he gets about £4 to £5 a week. I found out about the strike a couple of days ago, when I went in to send a telegram. He apologised profusely, and told me they were on strike.

We are going to the BMA meeting this week, leaving on Friday, 15th February, and returning on Wednesday, 20th February. It will be nice to get away for a little change.

I do not expect that we will be in Assam this time next year, but our plans for the future are very much in mid-air. Nonetheless, we are looking forward to a good holiday in the summer of 1958.

Our wireless aerial fell down a week ago, so we have had to tie it up in the most peculiar manner you ever saw. It is still picking up London, however, without any bother. The record player is also working very nicely.

Our strawberries are ripe just now. All the servants' children have been appearing in the last few days, to have a taste when we are not looking, but we do not have the heart to chase them. I got a strawberry barrel made by knocking holes in an old forty-gallon drum. The plants are now flowering furiously, and we are hoping to have strawberries during the hot season, because in the barrel they will not get waterlogged.

Mum

I remember the barrel. It was a good idea, and it meant we had fruit during the monsoon.

Dufflaghur Tea Estate, 23rd February 1957

The BMA meeting at Panitola (near Dibrugarh) was a great success. They even elected me to the council for the ensuing year!

BMA Meeting at Panitola in 1957
Seated 2nd from right: Dr Gilroy, Honorary Secretary
Standing 5th from right: Dad

The medical set-up of the tea gardens in that area is vastly superior to conditions here. They have a beautiful central hospital with facilities to do everything. They took me into theatre to see a partial gastrectomy (removal of stomach), and the improvement in theatre techniques since I was in hospitals, ten years ago, was amazing. They even got a cataract case in to show me the operation, so that I could do some here. Cataracts are exceedingly common in India.

We spent a day on the river, having sailed down in a locally-made boat with outboard engine, and enjoyed a curry on the river bank. Afterwards, we got a lift to Jorhat with one of the doctors, returning to his practice by car. Mrs Gilroy was not able to attend the meeting owing to a stomach upset, and Dr Gilroy had gone away early. She was all right by the time we reached Jorhat, however, and we were well looked after during our stay with them.

The meeting was a great tonic to us. Unfortunately, when we arrived at Jorhat, I discovered that I had left my briefcase at Panitola. To make matters worse, the postal strike in Assam had lasted six days, and I had been unable to post my letters before leaving for the meeting, so I took them with me in the briefcase. No doubt the briefcase will turn up quite soon, but until it arrives, I cannot post the letter I wrote to you before this one!

At Jorhat, we met an American official, who is doing a "fact-finding" tour of India to assess the expenditure by India of American aid towards the control of malaria, on a national basis. The assistant director of the Malaria Institute of India and an old colleague of Dr Gilroy's from Nigeria, accompanied him. It was in Nigeria that Dr Gilroy got his OBE for his work in malaria control, during and after the war. They were consulting Dr Gilroy regarding the position of tea gardens, while passing through, and also paying a visit to the Kaziranga Wildlife Reserve, which is about one hundred miles from Jorhat, where they saw elephants and rhinos.

Mum

I remember Panitola and the lovely curry on the river bank. I wouldn't be at the actual meeting – that was just the doctors. The wives would be together, and visits would be arranged. In Jorhat, we stayed with the Gilroys on many occasions, and they were very kind to us. I don't remember the incident with the briefcase, but I do recall an occasion Allan lost his wallet. Fortunately, it was found.

Dufflaghur Tea Estate, 23rd March 1957

We were pleased to receive your letters, and wish to apologise for taking so long to reply. I always appear to get myself cluttered up with clerical jobs, one way or another, until I cannot see over the pile. I wrote to the agents to say that I will not be renewing my agreement, but that we would like to stay on until March 1958. This would allow us six months' leave during the good weather at home, and not in the middle of winter. I have no idea what we might be doing after that. Mr Williamson wrote a personal letter, regretting that we would be leaving, and asking whether we might consider a practice in another area of Assam. I do not see that there would really be much difference. There are a small handful of practices where the facilities are good, but there are no openings there at the present moment. I also had a letter from Dr Gilroy, who met Dr Hay Arthur in Calcutta. The latter expressed regret that we were going, as he had thought I would take over from him when he retired. I think, for the moment at any rate, I have had more than a sufficiency of tea gardens.

The new manager and his wife (John and Joy Leitch) at Dufflaghur have settled in. He is very co-operative. Reita has a lovely crop of sweet peas this year. She got the gardeners to dig a huge trench, and replaced the sand (on which we are sitting) with good soil. The result has been excellent. There are lots of flowers, although not the quality of the ones at home. We can only eat a small proportion of the tomatoes that the gardeners are bringing in. They are all grown in the open. The strawberries are in full fruit, and the peas are ready for eating.

The malaria control programme is again in full swing. Dr Gilroy has promised to come over for a few days, about June, to see how we are getting on. He is going to bring Mrs Gilroy with him.

Mum

I don't know the full background regarding Allan's attempts to develop an efficient hospital and laboratory, but they were certainly never built in our area. He never discussed it in detail with me, but I know he got fed up with the battle of trying to push things forward to obtain adequate funding for medical developments, in general.

Dufflaghur Tea Estate, 7th April 1957

The weather is beginning to get warmer now, and I hope the Boroi Bridge will see us through May this year. It was washed away very early last year. I am going to see the income tax people in Tezpur quite soon. It seems I will have to get a clearance certificate from them for each year I have been working here, and that this will take months. The sooner I start, the better.

We are going down to Bishnauth tomorrow evening, to have dinner with Dr and Mrs Chopra. They always make us feel welcome when we are passing through. He qualified in Edinburgh a long time ago, and then took his DTM and DPH in Liverpool, before returning to India.

I have given your address to a young Indian couple, who are going on leave to the UK this year. He is an assistant manager on one of the tea gardens. His uncle was Finance Minister of India for a short time, and her father is an MP in Delhi. The name is Eappen.

We have had a letter from Dr Chesshire from his new practice on the south bank. His wife is due to arrive by sea quite soon, and he seems to like his new district.

Dufflaghur Tea Estate, 28th April 1957

Thank you for your letters. We are getting on quite well, and hope that Pop is now better after his bad asthmatic attack, and that his skin is improving. When he gets a bad spell with difficult breathing, he should rest very quietly, until it passes off. By this means, he is substantially reducing his requirements of oxygen during the period that the lungs are temporarily finding difficulty in supplying oxygen to the body.

The Church of Scotland minister and his wife (Mr and Mrs Nelson) stayed with us for a couple of days when he was doing a service at the club (Halem). The children, a boy of six and a little girl of two, were very amusing. The older boy, aged about eight years, is staying with his uncle, a minister at Barr, near Girvan. Mrs Nelson teaches the children herself, and obviously spends a great deal of valuable time on their education.

She recently spent five days in France, and the Reverend Donald Caskie, Paris minister, arranged accommodation for her. Her people were missionaries in China for a long time, until the communists took over.

We are thinking about doing a trip to Japan and back, while we are in this part of the world. After finishing here, we would do the trip and then return home, preferably by large cargo ship, to get a good view of all the parts on our way home. I am going to write to the shipping agencies for particulars. My agents in Calcutta will be able to help with arrangements. They have agreed to let me stay on until March 1958.

About a week ago, there was a very difficult maternity case at the Dufflaghur Hospital – a transverse lie, which is an insuperable obstruction to delivery, and meant mutilation of the infant. However, the mother did very nicely. A few days later, another patient was admitted with the same complaint (after hiding in the line until the last moment); unfortunately, she died ten minutes after admission, due to exhaustion, before we could do anything for her.

Today, we had a deputation at the bungalow (husband and relatives of the first woman), who insisted on washing our feet and presenting us with mutton and rice. It was a most touching and humbling ceremony to show their appreciation.

Mum

I remember the family coming to the bungalow. It was very moving.

The Nelson children were very well mannered – and a credit to their mother. Allan mentions that the Reverend Donald Caskie arranged accommodation for her. He was a very interesting man. He was from Islay, and was known as the "Tartan Pimpernel" for the work he did helping British soldiers escape from occupied France during the war. He wrote a book about it ("The Tartan Pimpernel" by Donald Caskie). Funnily enough, his mother was a great friend of my mother's, for they used to dig the peat together.

Dufflaghur Tea Estate, 18th May 1957

Dr Gilroy wrote a few days ago. He wants me to publish the malaria control results in this practice, so that it will be on permanent record. He would also like me to do some research in co-operation with him during the present rains. He says that it would create WHO interest, and should I decide to return to the Tropics (which is unlikely) it would no doubt be helpful.

Dufflaghur Tea Estate, 1st June 1957

The Boroi Bridge was washed away last Tuesday, which is exactly one month later than last year. This means the usual waiting and wading to get across on the little boat, twice a week. During May, we had rain practically every day. Last Saturday, however, it started fairly heavily, then on Sunday, 1.5 inches, on Monday, 1.75 inches, and on Tuesday, 1.25 inches. When I was returning on the little boat on Thursday afternoon, the river had again subsided, so that the boat stuck on a sandbank, twenty yards from this side. I had to wade up to the waist to get out of this predicament.

We have a serious outbreak of rinderpest in the locality, at the moment. I heard that a Nepali chap in the village had lost two hundred buffalo. In the tea garden itself, every animal attacked has died, especially the buffalo, which appears to have very little resistance to infection. The Government veterinary assistant has been doing mass inoculation of cattle, which should bring it to a halt. Unfortunately, the vaccine is so strong that one in every two hundred of the cattle dies of the inoculation.

Mum

I don't remember the buffalo dying. It was such a common occurrence for animals to die out there. What I do recall are the big birds like seagulls, only black in colour, that used to sit on the backs of the buffalo. Any time I went across to the Pattullos' bungalow, I always passed the buffalo and these horrible birds. I was always wary of the buffalo, but they really weren't interested in us at all.

I remember one time Allan had to wade across the river. I'd just had my lunch, and I was having a lie-back. I woke up and found Allan lying soaking wet on the floor. I thought he was dead! When I realised that he was sleeping, I called in the "pani wallah", and he prepared a bath. We got him fed and put him to bed. He was exhausted. I got an awful fright, and gave him such a row afterwards, for being so stupid!

Dufflaghur Tea Estate, 24th June 1957

We have had a very alarming time over the last week. The Indian manager (Mr Dam) on the tea garden next to us (Bormahjan) was beaten up by a small section of the garden labour on Tuesday (18th June), and sustained a fractured skull, from which he died the following day. I took him over to Jorhat, on the other side of the river, by light plane, but it was in vain.

The armed police came in force, and have arrested fifty-seven people. The tea garden has been closed from today, except for the hospital and maintenance in the factory. This is the third murder within a year, and the authorities feel that drastic action is necessary. The tea garden will probably remain closed until the cold weather. The dispute was about the amount of hoeing that constitutes a day's work, and was not a very serious point of dispute. The manager's wife was terribly upset. She could not fly over the same day, as the plane is too small, and had to go the following day, but he had died about an hour before her arrival. The local managers are feeling very fed-up with the whole affair.

I had a letter from Dr Hay Arthur in West Bengal. Reita and I paid a visit to his practice (which is a very good one, with X-rays, etc) in 1953. As he is retiring next year, he wanted me to take over his practice. He has a good air-conditioned operating theatre, with a fully qualified Indian assistant to help with the surgical work. The offer seemed very tempting, but it would still mean staying in the jungle (although not as bad as here). In any case, I have refused it, as we feel that we have had enough. Mr Dam's death has certainly removed any doubts we might have had. We had a letter from Dr Gilroy to say that Dr O J S McDonald (not Professor Macdonald), the Ross Institute representative in Ceylon, will be retiring in 1958 or 1959, and has asked for the name of a suitable man to succeed him. This is a very tempting offer, indeed. If the terms are good, we might give it a try for a year or two. It is also a very responsible job. Dr O J S McDonald's book on sanitation for rural areas is a classic. I would be a very poor substitute for him. Dr Gilroy is going to pay us a visit next month, and will be able to give us full particulars.

Mum

I remember Mr Dam's murder very well. It was terrible, and it was impossible to console Mrs Dam, who was a lovely lady, but had no English. I remember blood pouring out of Mr Dam's ears, nose and mouth. He was unconscious, but making gurgling noises, and never regained consciousness. The labour force had pelted him with bricks, and there was blood everywhere. I used to worry that something would happen to Allan when he was out and about doing his business, and can see now, from the letters, that Allan himself, was also concerned.

Dufflaghur Tea Estate, 16th July 1957

Many thanks for your letter. We were glad to hear that you enjoyed your holiday in St Andrews, and that Pop did not burn the bottom of the pots when you were away!

Dr and Mrs Gilroy are coming over for a few days, next week. I have started a malaria survey here, on behalf of the Ross Institute, and we will be publishing a joint report after it has been completed.

I had a letter from Professor Macdonald giving details of the Ceylon job. It is an administrative and advisory job. Because there is no clinical work (dealing with patients), I have turned it down, as I feel that I have not yet seen nearly enough clinical material. Professor Macdonald advised me to think hard, as it would mean a complete change of outlook. I have no idea what we will do when we leave Assam, but am not too worried. With my experience to-date, I should get a responsible job.

The neighbouring tea garden is still closed down, with the exception of essential facilities (hospital, factory maintenance, etc). The court proceedings should take place within a month. In all, eighty people have been arrested.

The Boroi River is cutting away the bank very badly at one side, this year. It carried away a huge tree to which the telegraph line had been temporarily attached. However, the repairs will no doubt be complete in a day or two.

Dufflaghur Tea Estate, 29 July 1957

We had Dr and Mrs Gilroy from Tuesday to Friday of last week, and enjoyed their visit very much. We have already started a little bit of research in this practice on behalf of the Ross Institute. At the present moment, I am sending about 150 blood slides to his laboratory, every week. These are for infants born this year, who could not have been infected with malaria in any previous year.

In this practice, ten years ago, the infant parasite rate was probably about 60%. To-date, however, none of the films has been positive. Afterwards, Dr Gilroy and I will publish a joint report regarding our findings. In the meantime, I am preparing a report regarding the methods used to control malaria in this practice over the last ten years, and especially over the last few years.

I am quite sure of getting a job with WHO at any time, as a malariologist, but am not keen on any job that would necessitate giving up clinical work. No doubt, I will end up in general practice at home, but the practice position should be better after 1958 when some of the older practitioners, who have been hanging on to complete the ten years required for pension, might finally decide to retire.

Our radio packed in last week. We were listening to it, and it was raining very heavily outside at the same time. Suddenly, there was a terrific flash of lightning, and it went out of action immediately – probably fuses or resistances. However, I have had a letter from Tezpur to say that it has been repaired, and the cost will be Rs 25/-. The first vehicle going into Tezpur from one of the tea gardens on the other side of the river, can pick it up for me.

We are expecting to leave for Japan about February 1958. After our return, we hope to get a freight passage from Calcutta.

Mum

The radio was always packing in – and there was a lot of thunder and lightning.

Dufflaghur Tea Estate, 17th August 1957

The agents are going to try to obtain a ship for us, leaving Calcutta towards the end of February 1958, for Japan. It will be a cargo ship and because of its great number of stops on the way, it will take two and a half months to complete the return journey. After that, we hope to get a cargo ship from Calcutta to the UK.

The weather has been very hot this month because of the reduction of rainfall. Our epidemic of Asiatic influenza has just cleared up. It ran a very abrupt course for three to four weeks, and then disappeared as quickly as it came. I was in bed for two days, but soon felt all right again.

Mrs Dam, the wife of the manager who was murdered, arrived back on the tea garden for a few days, last week, to clear up her belongings. We went down to see her, and she seemed quite bright, but was rather tearful as we were leaving. She was profuse with thanks for what we had done to help.

The court action has not yet started, and I am quite pleased because the Boroi River has been so difficult this year. The tea garden (Bormahjan) is now working normally again, but there will be a great reduction of crop because the garden was closed for a month. The growth, during this period, has had to be cut off and discarded, as only five to seven days leaf is of any value to making tea with the temperatures prevailing at present. It was also too high for the women to pluck.

We are going over to Jorhat for a few days in October, in connection with the centenary of the birth of Ronald Ross, who discovered the role of the mosquito in malaria transmission – hence the Ross Institute. Our research job for the Ross Institute in this practice, is doing nicely. We are following the amount of malaria transmission taking place, and Dr Gilroy will come over again in December, after the survey has been completed.

Dufflaghur Tea Estate, 8th September 1957

It will not be very long until we are on the high seas for Japan. We have a provisional booking on the "Santhia", leaving Calcutta on 28th

February (1958). The round trip takes about two and a half months, calling at many ports, and a full ten days in Japan. Our heavy baggage can be stored in Calcutta (with the agents) until we return from Japan. We have no booking as yet from Calcutta to the UK, but will no doubt manage to get this fixed up in due course. We are going to Tezpur on Tuesday, and will probably not get back until Thursday.

Medical evidence for the murder case (Mr Dam) is being taken on Wednesday, 11th September. My summons to court arrived last week.

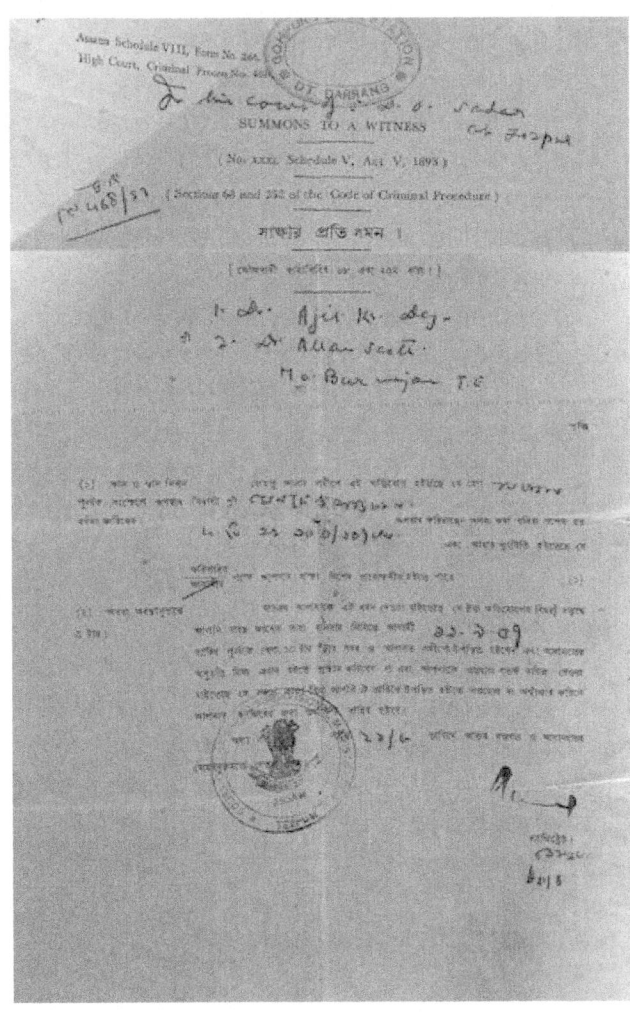

Citation in Hindi Script

It was written in Hindi script, and I had to get it translated as I cannot read a word of script. This is the Lower Court hearing. Later, further evidence will be required at the High Court. It is a good job we did not decide to leave at the beginning of November, as the case might go on until then.

Our malaria survey is still going on smoothly. I am also preparing two other preparatory papers for publication. Dr Gilroy feels that it would be a pity not to publish the practice results over the last six years, in addition to the present survey.

Tomorrow will be your (Mother) sixty-third birthday. Reita joins with me in sending our best wishes and many happy returns.

We were over at the wedding reception of Dr Chopra's daughter, last week, at Bishnauth. It was a great splash, and thoroughly enjoyed by all. The young couple are now staying on this side of the river. He is an Indian assistant manager on one of the tea gardens in the practice.

Dinko Chopra and Mahendra Singh get married

Left to right: Charles MacCarthy (tea planter), Dinko, Mahendra, Babs MacCarthy (Charles MacCarthy's wife) and Mrs Chopra (bride's mother) Sitting: Dr Chopra (bride's father)

Left to right: Mahendra, Mum, Bill Adams (tea planter) and Dad

We had the Scottish minister (Mr Nelson) staying with us for two days, when he was giving a service at the club. He has very kindly offered to put us up for a few days at Jorhat, when we go over to the centenary celebrations of the birth of Ronald Ross. Dr and Mrs Gilroy will be feeding sixty or seventy people at their bungalow, where everything will be taking place.

Mum

I remember the wedding very well. The groom was a lovely boy. He was from Rajasthan. I liked him very much. In fact, I could have fallen for him, myself – but he was only a boy!

Dufflaghur Tea Estate, 29th September 1957

We had a wire from Edinburgh, the week before last, to say that Reita's sister, Annie, had died suddenly in Edinburgh Royal Infirmary. This was followed by an airmail letter, which said she had died as the result of a stomach complaint.

In three weeks, the night temperature will be right down. It is still very hot at the present moment. There were seven inches of rain between Wednesday evening and midday on Thursday. I had to stay put on Thursday, until the bridges (road) had been repaired.

Two weeks ago, I was at court giving evidence about the murder. The eighty arrested people were jammed into the courtroom, roped and handcuffed together, so that they could hear the proceedings. As this was the Lower Court hearing, there was little cross-examination. I will have to go at a later date to give evidence at the High Court.

Mum

Annie's husband wrote to tell us what had happened. We found out later that she also had a bad ulcer on one of her legs, and the start of ovarian cancer.

Dufflaghur Tea Estate, 20th October 1957

We were very pleased to receive your letters. I do not quite know what I will do when we get back home. I shall probably go into hospital for six months, with a view to the DRCOG (Diploma of the Royal College of Obstetricians and Gynaecologists). With the help of this, it should be easier to get straight into a good practice, without having to do assistantships for years on end. The DRCOG is not excessively difficult, but one must have done one year of post-graduate hospital work, of which, six months must be in obstetrics. It is a much easier diploma than the MRCOG (Member of the Royal College of Obstetricians and Gynaecologists), which requires four years doing obstetrics in hospital.

Dr Chopra went away for two weeks leave last Saturday. I have had to go to Bishnauth four times for urgent cases. His farthest garden is over fifty miles from here, so I am hoping I don't get a call there.

The monsoon is almost finished, and the evenings are much cooler. The piles for the temporary bridge over the River Boroi are now halfway across. The bridge should be ready in three weeks.

Mum

That damned bridge! It was always a "temporary" bridge – when it was there, that is! It was very bumpy. I'm in a wheelchair now, and I'm jolly glad I wasn't then. We never managed to see the permanent bridge – we left before it was built. I used to call it: "the bridge that never was".

Dufflaghur Tea Estate, 7th November 1957

The temporary Boroi Bridge was opened yesterday, which will be a great help.

The research job with the Ross Institute is now almost finished. The conclusion is already obvious. Apart from the stray carrier blown in, and the occasional man going out, which will always happen at present, but is not important, transmission on the tea garden is virtually nil. I will be writing this up as a report, jointly, with Dr Gilroy. The journal of Tropical Hygiene has accepted a paper from me regarding the Assam influenza, which struck us about four months ago. The journal is edited by Ross Institute Headquarters in London.

Late last night, I got an urgent call to see the pharmacist on one of the tea gardens. He was returning home after visiting some friends (on his bicycle), and was attacked by two bears. We got his extensive injuries attended to last night, but his general condition is still very critical, due to shock and blood loss. If he survives today, he will probably be all right. It is about two years since we had a case of bear injuries, and these are usually very serious.

The BMA got a small issue of polio vaccine. I got eight courses, which I am in the process of giving.

The hearing of the homicide case, at which I gave evidence, has been referred to the High Court. In all, there are sixty-two labourers still under arrest. This will mean giving further evidence when the High Court judge comes round.

Mum

I don't remember that particular bear incident, but I did see others. They were really awful. The bear would more or less remove the face of the victim, and scalp them. It was usually the women, who were plucking the tea, who were attacked. We never got a decent hospital, and they would have to lie on the floor, instead of a bed, with their family looking after them, and all their young children would be tripping around in a most unsuitable environment.

Dufflaghur Tea Estate, 20th November 1957

We are off tomorrow morning for Tezpur, and after spending one night there, will cross to the south bank and on to Jorhat. We have decided to stay at the Indian Tea Association guest house in Jorhat, but will stay one night at the wild game reserve (Kaziranga Reserve), so we can go out on the elephant at first light to see the animal life. Mr Nelson (Scots minister) has already attended to all the arrangements on our behalf. Since we are due two weeks' leave for

1957, we have decided to go on to Shillong after the Ross Centenary function.

I am working on two reports just now – one on malaria and one on eye diseases – which I hope to publish in January, in addition to the joint report with Dr Gilroy.

Mum

I remember the Kaziranga Reserve. In fact, I'll never forget it! I understand it's all changed now, but when we were there, it was unforgettable. The people were very nice, but the accommodation not so. We stayed in a shack with two small beds. I ended up with Allan in his bed because the ground was covered in scurrying rats.

We arose very early the next morning, before it was light, and took a trip on the elephants, through the reserve. The "Mahout" (man guiding the elephant) was on the elephant with us. We were on a sort of wooden board. I was in the middle, hanging on to him for dear life, whilst Allan sat behind me – hanging on to me for dear life. We were there to see the rhinos, and we were in among them. It was actually quite dangerous because they would charge if they thought their young were in any danger. Fortunately, there were no incidents.

Dufflaghur Tea Estate, 9th December, 1957

We enjoyed the Ronald Ross Centenary function very much – and also our visit to the Kaziranga Reserve. We went out on one of the elephants at first light and saw eight rhinos and some hog deer, but the trip itself on the elephant was the most enjoyable. We went through small rivers, over marshes and through grass, up to the level of our shoulders, as we sat on the elephant. The forest officer who travelled with us was saying that he had gone out on the same elephant, a week or so previously, to supervise grass cutting on the reserve, and a female rhino had charged the elephant, which took fright, bolted and threw both himself and the young boy with him to the ground. However, they got themselves picked up, and no harm was done. The first rhino that we saw was another angry female, so we steered off. Others, in small groups, were quite happy when we went right up to them. Afterwards, we made our way to Shillong, which was very cold indeed.

Tell Pop that the pharmacist is now much better. Unfortunately, the same pair of bears attacked two women when I was away. Luckily, these attacks were not so serious.

Dufflaghur Tea Estate, 24th December 1957

Dr and Mrs Chesshire are coming over to this area for Christmas. They will be staying with some friends at Bishnauth. We are going to Bishnauth (tomorrow) to a Christmas party at the club, and will stay one night with the assistant manager at Monabarie Tea Estate (Roy and Caroline Eastment).

I have just returned from Nya Gogra (twenty miles the opposite way), after seeing a case of obstructed labour, but as the patient is not yet ready, I will have to go out in the early morning to get her delivery completed. I always seem to get a difficult maternity case at Christmas or the New Year.

We are getting quite excited now at the prospect of finishing up, but I still have three papers to complete. At the moment, each of the tea gardens is making a wooden trunk for me to pack all our belongings for the homeward journey. It is amazing the amount of stuff one gathers, as the years go past.

We have a Dumbarton couple managing this tea garden just now. He is acting manager (Mr and Mrs McHard – her own name is Irene Gordon). They have a little girl called Marilyn, who is on the tea garden at present, on holiday from school in Darjeeling. The children have their long holiday at Christmas in Assam, and carry on with their schooling in the hill stations during the hot weather.

We are expecting another batch of Glaxo Polio vaccine within a week or two. The previous injections have done very well.

I am expecting a summons to court (any day now) to give further evidence in the homicide case. It should be finished by the end of January.

Mum

Funnily enough, the McHards had gone to the school in Dumbarton, where Allan's Uncle Jim (James Harvey Scott) taught them music. They told us that Jim's nickname at the school was: "Big Zeek"!

18

JANUARY TO MAY 1958

Dufflaghur Tea Estate, 14th January 1958

We are now making preparations for our departure. We will be leaving the tea garden about 22nd February, and sailing from Calcutta on the "Santhia" (British India Steam Navigation Co – subsidiary company of P&O) on 28th February. We will have ten days in Japan, using the ship as a hotel, and will return to Calcutta on 29th April. We are then hoping to get a freighter from Calcutta, so that there will not be too much difficulty in regard to baggage, but we have no definite confirmation of this, at present. We will probably have two weeks in Calcutta.

Ten days ago, I had a letter from the agents, offering new terms if I would stay on. They suggested I take leave, as usual, and then communicate with them after I have seen how things are at home. However, I have not promised to return to Assam. I still intend going into hospital (for six months) to take the DRCOG – and also to get the Assam cobwebs blown out of my hair.

Dufflaghur Tea Estate, 1st February 1958

The agents have not as yet managed to get anyone to take my place. There are rumours that a locum will be appointed to begin with. We will be leaving Assam, three weeks from today.

I got a summons to the Session Court to give medical evidence on 28th January, but this has been postponed. I am hoping to get this part finished next week.

We have completed our vaccinations and inoculations. I had a terrific reaction to the second TAB and Cholera, shivering violently for six to eight hours, with a temperature of 103 F. That was on Thursday. By yesterday, I was feeling much better – and today I am quite all right.

Mum

Every time Allan had an injection, he reacted badly. I remember he was very ill on that occasion.

Grand Hotel, Calcutta, 27th February 1958

Many thanks for your letters. I am sorry to have taken so long to write. With our packing, and my paper on malaria control, it has been a terrific rush. I got the paper posted on 22nd February, which was the day we left the tea garden.

Before we left, we got a presentation. A silver cigarette case each, and a silver cigarette box for the table. The planters at the club gave us an informal send-off.

We have been staying at the Grand Hotel (Calcutta), and our ship sails this afternoon. We have a booking by the Scindia Line, leaving Calcutta on 9th May for the UK. It will probably take about six to seven weeks to get home. I shall write from the ship.

Mum

I don't remember Allan finally having to give evidence. He can't have been required because we left. But I do know that the accused labourers were sentenced to life imprisonment on the Andaman Islands.

Santhia, 19th March 1958

We are having a very enjoyable trip, and expect to reach Hong-Kong at 3.30pm today. Rumour has it that there are quite a few expelled Chinese on board (down below), who will go straight for Red China, and will be most carefully watched to make sure they do not stay at Hong-Kong. Rangoon, Penang and Singapore were very hot.

We are now a good bit further north again, and the weather is much cooler. The ship is rolling a bit today for the first time during our voyage, and the wind is blowing with some rain. By the time we get to Japan, it will definitely be warm clothes, and by the time we get back to Rangoon and Calcutta, it will be the hottest time of the year.

At Singapore, a young Jewish doctor (doing his national service) and his wife came on. They are doing a trip to Japan and back, which takes a month from Singapore. Also on board, is an Indian couple. They have been all over Europe, but never out this way before, and are good company. Another Indian couple are on board, and we have got to know them. He is the Aga Khan's personal representative for Calcutta, and he has people meeting him at every port.

The crew are all very nice. We have been entertained in their cabins, seen through the engine room, etc. We know the engineers particularly well because we share the same table with them for meals.

Mum

When we got to the port at Rangoon, we were all made to pay a fee before we were allowed on land. It was there I bought my ivory ornaments. When we were in Penang, Allan and I were swimming in the sea. We only found out later that it was dangerous to do that. Not only that, I got sunburnt, and the captain of the "Santhia" gave me a telling off!

We did not see much of the Aga Khan's personal assistant, since he was always doing business, but I got to know his wife very well. She couldn't speak English, but I still managed to teach her how to play cards. We played "Spite and Malice" and "Canasta". I was always the best at cards but eventually she got so good, she started to beat me.

Santhia, 9 April 1958

When we left Hong-Kong, on our way to Japan, we were stopped by a Chinese nationalist war ship at 2am. It was lying in complete darkness, and suddenly shot out a signal for our ship to stop, but since we were going pretty fast at the time, we had to circle round it to acknowledge its signal, and then we were given permission to proceed.

The holiday in Japan was really lovely, apart from the climate during the first three or four days, when it snowed. From Yokohama, we did day trips, and got round quite a bit of country in the electric trams, which are just as good as the tram services at home – possibly even better. Everyone travels by tram, and buses take secondary place as a means of transport in Japan. Car hiring is very expensive.

The day we went up to Lake Chuzenji (4,000 feet), it started to snow. Not having much heavy clothing with us, we felt the cold considerably. By the time we got back to Tokyo, the snow had turned into sleet, and we had rapidly to buy an umbrella to protect us. Fortunately, some shops in Japan stay open until 9pm, so we had no difficulty in making our purchases.

From Kobe, we did the same sort of thing, and went one day to a very famous theatre, where the "show" was really lovely. About three-quarters of the way through, however, the "show" was stopped, and we discovered later that one of the girls had been killed in the machinery of one of the elevating floors of the stage, as she went off. We did not see anything, as the part of the stage where it happened was below the general level. It was the first time anything like this had happened in the theatre's forty years of existence.

Mum

I remember the accident. We were sitting next to an English lady in the theatre, and she had an interpreter with her who was able to tell us that the Japanese girl had been wearing a very wide dress on stage, and as she descended, the dress got caught in the machinery, and she was killed.

Calcutta, 2nd May 1958

On the way back from Japan, we returned to Singapore and went out to dinner with the young Jewish doctor and his wife, who are stationed there. He is expecting his discharge quite soon.

There was another army doctor (and his wife), and on their arrival at Singapore they discovered they only had two days in which to pack for his transfer to Kuala Lumpur.

The Jewish couple have a tape recorder, and do all their correspondence by voice. It was most amazing to hear one's own voice recorded back again. If I had had more information, I would probably have bought one in Hong-Kong.

In Hong-Kong, we bought a large, camphor wood chest and teak cocktail cabinet, which were going for a song. The carving is really first class.

Chest

Cocktail Cabinet

We arrived back in Calcutta on 29th April, after a most enjoyable trip. It will stand in our memories for ever. It is so nice to have seen a place, when everyone talks about it. We have met several people from Assam passing through, since we arrived. Our new ship is the "Jaladharma" (Scindia Line – an Indian shipping line), and it leaves Calcutta between 2nd and 9th May. I do not know the ports of call.

Mum

The "Jaladharma" was a cargo ship, and was destined for South India.

Jaladharma, 13th May 1958

A few days after the "Santhia" arrived in Calcutta, the Customs discovered gold bullion, worth £30,000, on board. The ship is now practically under arrest. As nobody will be proved responsible (in all probability), the ship will be heavily fined. She was due to sail on 9th May, but this will set her back a week or ten days.

Our new ship, "MV Jaladharma", is very comfortable – cabin with bathroom attached. The captain is British, but all other members of the crew are Indian. There are six passengers in addition to ourselves, two of whom, are children.

After London, the ship will visit Liverpool and then Glasgow, and we are hoping to get our nine crates of heavy baggage taken to Glasgow, which would be a great help.

At the moment, the ship has called in at Vizagapatam, which is half-way between Calcutta and Madras, to pick up manganese ore for Glasgow. Blue Funnel Line had no ship on the spot, and chartered this ship to take the ore at the last minute.

We leave here tomorrow afternoon, and then on to Cochin in South India. Unfortunately, we will not be able to see Ceylon, as the ship has no cargo to or from Colombo. After Cochin, the only stops are Aden (six hours only) and Port Said (twelve hours only), and then on to London about 14th June.

It was terribly hot when we were in Calcutta, and we were quite pleased to get on board the "Jaladharma", and make our way down the Hooghly River. It is also hot here, but there is a bit of a breeze in the evening. By the time we get into the Mediterranean, the weather should be excellent.

Mum

We were very surprised to hear about the gold bullion. Apparently, we were sitting on seats, stuffed with gold, which was stashed all over the ship. If only we'd known!

Jaladharma, 14th May 1958

Our departure has been delayed from this afternoon to tomorrow morning. We will probably reach Cochin on Sunday morning. By the time I get home, after three and a half months at sea, I should be able to qualify for a seaman's certificate??!! It has been very nice and interesting to see so many parts of the world.

Mum

We ate and drank like royalty – and were attended to, hand and foot. It was an experience I have never forgotten.

Cochin, 24th May 1958

We have had some delay here, and will not be sailing until tomorrow. I did not think it would take us so long to get out of India. Our arrival date in London had been changed from 7th to 14th June, but this will not be possible now, as there is some talk of picking up cargo in Port Sudan.

However, when we do get underway, the ship is very fast (seventeen knots), and should be able to catch up with some of the delay. I think it is going to be possible to have our nine heavy crates unloaded at Glasgow, instead of London. The shipping company has been very good to us at the ports. Having offices at ports, they have been able to lay on car runs for us with the captain or first officer.

The captain is retiring after this trip. This is the second time he has retired – the last time being in the Royal Navy, nine years ago. A Mr and Mrs Weeks share a table with us in the dining room. He was originally a ship's officer, and then took on a job as pilot and harbour master in Calcutta. From there, he joined the Bengal Chamber of Commerce in their shipping department, and is now giving up his work in India.

The chief officer is a young Indian chap from the Punjab, and he has been very good in keeping us entertained. Mr and Mrs Cooper and two children are probably of mixed blood, and are settling down in the UK for good. They have relatives in London.

We will be quite pleased when the ship gets under way again, as the heat is really oppressive, especially in the late afternoon. By 5pm, we will take a walk to the local hotel, which has a swimming pool, and have a dip.

As we pass through the Mediterranean, we will have to do a bit of sunbathing to have a really good tan for our arrival home. At the moment, we are avoiding the sun as much as possible.

*

And that was the last of the letters...

Mum

That's the end? No more letters? Pity. I remember the car runs with the captain and first officer. We were taken to see places of interest. Allan and I also went to a mango grove in one of the ports of call. We got a load of mangoes, but they didn't last long in the heat.

I remember Mr and Mrs Weeks. They were a nice couple. I also remember the chief officer. I don't recall his name, but I used to play cards with him – and I always won! I don't remember too much about Mr and Mrs Cooper, only that they were very excited about going to London.

Our nine crates were delivered at Glasgow, but we had to get off at Liverpool and do the rest of the journey by train. When we arrived in Glasgow, disaster struck! Allan's mother was away on holiday, and his father succumbed to pneumonia. We looked after him, and because we didn't want to spoil Allan's mother's holiday, we told her on the phone that all was well.

Mistake!

Allan's father heard us, and was not amused: "God forgive you!" he cried. "Tell my wife she's to come home!"

We were stuck in the middle, but decided not to tell her. Fortunately, Allan's father got well, and his mother returned on her due date.

But let me just add, before finishing, for those who might be wondering, I'm pleased to say that Allan never did buy that bloody gun!

AFTERWORD AND APPENDICES

The letters had most certainly ended on a rather sudden note. What was more, after a sea of adventures, this abruptness seemed to spell disappointment. It made me feel sad, especially when I reflected on the fact that I had not known the full story of Mum and Dad's life in Assam, before Dad's death.

It was perhaps time to do a bit more digging – but first, an explanation of what happened next.

When Dad left India in 1958, he went on to work in hospitals, then general practice in Scotland, followed by the North of England. By 1961, he and Mum were parents to two girls: my sister (Désirée) and myself. Then in 1964, he got his Diploma in Obstetrics of the Royal College of Obstetricians and Gynaecologists (DObst RCOG).

Left to right: Désirée, Dad and me

When we moved to Rochester (Kent) in 1964, Dad joined a medical practice, and continued to work as a general practitioner. He remained there as a senior partner, until he was sadly diagnosed with Parkinson's disease when he was in his sixties. Despite the debilitating effects of the disease, my parents made efforts to continue enjoying life, and finally decided to move back to Glasgow, where my sister was studying medicine.

Dad is offering advice to Désirée on her graduation day

Enjoying a buffet at a family "do"

Unfortunately, the disease took its toll, and complications arose causing Dad to pass away in 2004. By this time, age was creeping up on Mum, and although I was her carer, I sometimes didn't know who was caring for whom. She did not like to stay in on a Friday night – whatever the weather!

Mum and me out dining (2018)

Mum and me "in our bubble" during Covid (2020)

Sadly, Mum passed away in 2021 (aged 98 years), but left behind a great legacy of tales, which included Assam and Dad's hard work and ultimate disappointments. Dad had been a pioneer – of that, I am certain. He had always gone the extra mile to ensure that everything ran smoothly, and had relied, where he could, on the support and encouragement of three experienced doctors: Dr Hay Arthur, Dr Gilroy and Professor Macdonald.

Dr Hay Arthur had fought over the years to get his hugely efficient hospital with X-ray equipment in Dooars, West Bengal. He even had a central laboratory. Dad had aspired to replicate these conditions in Dufflaghur, however, despite hard work, this dream never came to fruition.

Then there was Dr Gilroy (Principal of the India Branch of the Ross Institute of Tropical Hygiene, Assam), an Australian gentleman with whom Dad carried out research. The pair wrote a paper (in 1958) that was published in the Indian Journal of Malariology: *The Infant Parasite Rate on Some Assam Tea Estates.*

Finally, there was Professor Macdonald of the Ross Institute. Dad's letters had already indicated that:

"Professor Macdonald was for many years in Assam as a younger man, but now has his headquarters at London University for the branches all over the world. He did the WHO (World Health Organisation) report on malaria conditions in Korea last year – and incidentally, was the man who interviewed me for my present job."

A nice introduction, but I decided to delve deeper, and found more interesting information. His full name was Professor George Macdonald, and he had been Professor of Tropical Hygiene at the London School of Hygiene and Tropical Medicine – as well as director of the Ross Institute.

As I researched further, I uncovered facts showing that Professor Macdonald had been a dominant figure in the field of tropical public health. He'd been one of the world's great authorities of malariology, and had distinguished himself with his work on quantitative analysis of the transmission and eradication of vector-borne tropical diseases.

I further discovered that Professor Macdonald had worked with Sir Ronald Ross (whom Dad had also mentioned in his letters), collaborating with him in the development of a mathematical model of mosquito-borne pathogen transmission; and that the Ross Institute and Hospital for Tropical Medicine had been established in 1926 (named in Sir Ronald's honour), and later became part of the London School of Hygiene and Tropical Medicine.

I finally found that Professor Macdonald had died on 10th December 1967; and that in October 1968, a medal had been introduced in his memory. The medal is now awarded every three years to candidates in recognition of outstanding research leading to improvements in health in tropical countries.

In my opinion, three outstanding men – so what had gone wrong at Dufflaghur?

Challenges

The answer is probably too many challenges – and I have divided these into the following:

- (i) Existing medical conditions.
- (ii) Attitudes.
- (iii) Geography.
- (iv) Economics.

Existing medical conditions

It is clear that Dad reviewed the hospital situation at Dufflaghur very promptly, and by 1952 was initiating efforts to create good facilities (hospital, maternity units, X-ray unit and central laboratory).

"The tea garden I attended on Friday is the biggest in my district, and plans are going ahead for the construction of a maternity unit there. The plans have all been made to suit my suggestions, and it will give me great satisfaction to get this into proper working order after it has been built. This should be done next cold weather."

As time progressed, so did Dad's aspirations.

"By next cold weather, I now hope to have three maternity hospitals up and running, and have every normal case supervised by the trained midwife. These midwives are usually given a year's course of instruction at one of the mission hospitals, after which, they get a diploma. Given a proper chance, their results are really very good, and you can always be sure of a timely warning from them if anything goes wrong."

Unfortunately, "economic factors" put a stop to this.

"Since the fall in the price of tea, I have been answering letters from Williamson Magor regarding proposed cuts in hospital developments."

Mum was quick to comment:

"Yes – Allan was always being told to cut down on hospital development expenses, and it used to annoy him."

By 1953, things were not getting any better.

"I have a patient at the moment with a liver abscess. I have already drained two pockets of pus from her liver, but feel that she has another abscess forming in a different part of her liver. She came in at first with a severe pneumonia, then developed one abscess, which I drained between the ribs. The liver continued to enlarge, and I drained a further one with an upper abdominal incision, two weeks ago. She improved greatly after that, but her liver has started to enlarge again and her heart is beginning to fail. Her general condition was so poor, yesterday, when I saw her, that I decided to do nothing. She will probably die, as she cannot possibly stand much more of this sort of thing. There has been so much pus that I doubt there is much healthy liver tissue left. A portable X-ray would be just the thing for letting me know where and how many abscesses are present."

Unfortunately, nowhere in the letters does it say that he got a portable X-ray unit.

Towards the end of 1953, despite obstacles, Dad continued to pursue his medical objectives, and paid a visit to Dr Hay Arthur's practice in Dooars (West Bengal) to get more ideas in order to discuss medical improvements with the tea company in Calcutta.

"I visited Dr Hay Arthur's practice, and it was well worth the visit. He has a central hospital (with X-ray equipment) and a great organisation, extending out to his smallest dispensary. In my practice, when a patient comes into hospital, he or she brings the husband or wife to act as attendant, and usually half a dozen children have to be put up at the same time. This method is simply asking for a filthy state of affairs. In Dooars, this practice has been eliminated, and only the sick are allowed into hospital. He has trained some of the girls in the labour force to come in for nursing duties and organise the hospitals on lines similar to those at home. These nurses can take a temperature, record it on the chart, give an injection, etc, and the difference can only be described as amazing."

By February 1954, a new hospital seemed feasible.

"I have already designed a new hospital for Dufflaghur, and apart from some small technical alterations, this is now off to the architects, having been accepted. It will cost between £5,000 and £10,000, plus the extras later."

And by March 1954, Dad was pushing for a laboratory.

"I have got the plans for the central laboratory completed, and *these will be sent out for estimates. It is probably going to cost about £1,500 to £2,000 to get it functioning, and the agents have accepted this, in principle."*

However, by June 1954, the agents were clearly procrastinating.

"The prices of tea at the present moment, are beyond all expectation. I hope it will last for a wee while, as the agents have almost agreed to build me a laboratory, and supply me with some central staff for the practice. This would be a great help."

Sadly, going through all the letters, it is obvious that in the end Dad got none of the things he asked for – and there was certainly no hospital or laboratory ever built at Dufflaghur during his time there.

Mum summed it up:

"Allan really did have a problem in getting people interested in his medical projects, but kept pursuing them in the hope that he could improve medical conditions out there. Even when there was more money available, people were reluctant to use any of it for medical development. This upset Allan greatly."

Attitudes

The reluctance of the tea companies to improve medical conditions is spelled out throughout Dad's correspondence, rendering him frustrated and sad. Where other Europeans (managers, etc) were concerned, Dad claims not to have faced too much in the way of opposition, except from some of the older, less flexible tea planters.

"I have had one or two wee tiffs with some of the managers. They can be very exasperating. Each has his own wee area where his say is law, and sometimes they like to extend their orders to the visiting medical officer."

Mum was quick to corroborate this:

"Some of the managers wanted the Company to spend money on their things alone, and weren't interested in improving the medical service – so that could be a problem."

Fortunately, by 1954 the situation seems to have changed for Dad where the managers were concerned.

"I do not get much trouble nowadays in regard to medical policy, as most of the managers are only too anxious to get the best possible

results."

I wondered, however, how much this had to do with Dad's physical presence in India, since Mum later advised that not long after they left Assam, a new manager put in a request for a swimming pool, and the tea company granted it. I've no idea how much this luxury would have cost the tea company, but it was certainly a slap in the face for my father.

Geography

I would say that another great challenge must have been location. Dufflaghur is very remote, situated on the north bank of the Brahmaputra in upper north east Assam, close to the foothills of the Himalayas. Not only was his practice in the back of beyond, it contained some 26,000 people, covering an area as far away as forty miles. The fact it was split in two by the River Boroi did not help matters, and from the start Dad found himself wasting a lot of time and energy on travel – one of the reasons he wanted to create hospitals and units in his area with good facilities, so patients could get treated with little hindrance, and be dealt with in a timelier manner.

Cases, of course, became further complicated when facilities at Dufflaghur were insufficient, and he had to send patients to one of the big hospitals. Where the labour force was concerned, this would mean from twelve to sixteen hours on the night steamer, up and across the river.

The roads were certainly not ideal, especially during the monsoon. Mud, flooding and ruts in the road's surface all proved problematic.

"In this part of the world there are many little wooden bridges over deep ruts in the road that drain away the rain water during the monsoon, and when they take the bridges down to renew them, they do not always put up a sign or road block. In short, when the full significance of a particular rut in the road (about four feet broad by two feet deep) became obvious in the headlamps, it was too late to prevent ourselves going in with a bump."

Even in the cold weather, the roads became an issue.

"We have had the most unusual weather this year. The roads are

usually dry and very dusty at this time, but not this year. Can you imagine our plight? I have been careful in avoiding the possibility of getting stuck in the mud. I did not manage to get to the other end of my practice today, but got an urgent call to a more accessible part. The ruts on the road are anything up to a foot deep."

As for the temporary bamboo bridge over the River Boroi – that was something unto itself. Despite promises that it would be replaced by a permanent steel one, this certainly never happened during the time my parents were in Assam. Dad's reliance on the "ferry service" when the bridge was washed away during the monsoon, presented its own problems.

"Once the bridge goes, I will have to cross by ferry boat, and owing to the trouble involved with that, I will not be taking too many unnecessary journeys."

Issues intensified over the years.

"There is still no bridge between the two parts of my practice, and I have often been delayed with the ferry sticking in the shallow parts."

In August 1954, the monsoon was so bad it was reported on the BBC News.

"We are getting it very hot just now. Until a week ago, it rained every day, and the roads are in a terrible mess. Without the Land Rover, I could not have managed to get out to work on many occasions during July. We were astonished to hear "Assam" on the "BBC News", a couple of days ago. The mail buses and other vehicles have not been able to cross the Boroi River for about two weeks, owing to the very high level of the river, with tree trunks roaring down in the current. When I crossed today, it had decreased to a very small river again, but sandbanks had been deposited on one side, about fifty yards wide, and they were preparing a wire so that vehicles would be able to cross it. The sand was still soft today, and my legs were sinking up to the knees, trying to cross it at some parts."

Mum remembered these issues well, and was quick to comment:

"...we were always having problems on the road. There was always something happening to the Land Rover. If it wasn't the Land Rover, it was the road, which was nothing more than a dirt track. Many a night we were stranded till the morning."

She also recalled the promises of a new steel bridge, and summed the situation up well.

"That damned bridge! It was always a "temporary" bridge – when it was there, that is! It was very bumpy. I'm in a wheelchair now, and I'm jolly glad I wasn't then. We never managed to see the permanent bridge – we left before it was built. I used to call it: 'the bridge that never was'."

Economics

Dad was very clear in his letters about the inconsistencies of prices imposed by the different pharmaceutical companies, and how these differences impacted on his work.

"My biggest headache at the moment is trying to reduce the drug bill without upsetting treatment. I need to cut out the delicacies of treatment, the value of which is doubtful or temporary, and I have spent weeks on this."

Mum said this was a recurring theme. The tea companies wanted to cut costs, and the pharmaceuticals wanted to make money.

"Allan had his hands full. I remember him almost tearing his hair out trying to organise the drugs."

Dad further wrote:

"I am still doing the survey of medical costs to see if economies can be made. The bill for last year was Rs 60,000 to Rs 70,000 (roughly £5,000) for the district as a whole, and was even greater the previous year.

"It is a big job pricing the medicines to see which are the luxuries and which are not. I am trying to find which preparations are the best buy, and the differences in the prices of similar products out here are really terrific. Luminal (phenobarbitone made by Bayer) costs Rs 16 per ounce. Gardenal (phenobarbitone made by M&B) costs Rs 4 per ounce. You can see the difficulties involved when you consider that these two preparations are equally effective in treatment."

Promises

Although medical enthusiasm might have existed in Dad's small medical circle, the slow pace of the tea companies, provincial government and central government proved to be a constant headache for him. As I read the letters, my senses told me that for a while Dad truly believed he would achieve his goals: hospital, maternity units, X-ray units and well-equipped laboratory for blood analysis. He even appeared to be encouraged by the tea companies, until – nothing.

So, were the tea companies simply "dangling a carrot" with their promises? I remembered how abruptly Dad's correspondence had ended. His earlier letters had been full of aspirations, then as the years had passed, references had become fleeting, until there had been no mention of his dreams at all. It seemed to me that Dad had been propelled into unfamiliar territory, where he'd complied with requirements as far as he could, often going above and beyond, until in the end he was pushed too far – and realisation struck him: it wasn't going to happen.

I reflected long on how Dad must have felt during this time, and wondered if the difficulties he'd faced were simply signs of the time. How lovely it would be to find that now, in the twenty-first century, seventy years later, attitudes were different, allowing medical services to leap forward and provide excellent facilities for Dufflaghur and other remote tea gardens in Assam. Perhaps a state-of-the-art hospital and first-class central laboratory? I couldn't wait to research it; however, when I did, I discovered some disappointing facts.

Today's Remote Tea Estates

As Dad had indicated in his letters, Dufflaghur Tea Estate is situated in upper north east Assam, up against hills and jungle. It is very remote, and the nearest main town is Tezpur, which is about eighty-five miles away.

Dad spoke frequently about communications with the "agents", "firms" and the "Company", making reference, in particular, to George Williamson & Co, Williamson Magor and McLeod Russel. Mum indicated that they were all connected in some way, so I decided to do a spot of research into the Group.

Dufflaghur is currently owned by MacLeod Russel, which is part of the Williamson Magor Group. Williamson Magor dates back to 1866, and has undergone numerous structural changes. The Company is now located at 4 Mangoe Lane, Surendra Mohan Ghosh Sarani, Kolkata 700001, and is a major Group Shareholding Company, listed on the BSE (Bombay Stock Exchange), the National Stock Exchange of India, the Calcutta Stock Exchange and the Gauhati Stock Exchange. In other words, the Williamson Magor Group is a big, flourishing organisation.

Having established ownership of Dufflaghur Tea Estate, I then looked to see what recent steps have been taken to improve medical services, particularly, on tea estates as remotely situated as Dufflaghur. I discovered that the remote tea gardens, like Dufflaghur, now rely heavily on a Public-Private Partnership (PPP) initiative with the National Health Mission (NHM), which aims to provide healthcare services to tea estate employees. The scheme includes the use of Tea Garden Hospitals and Mobile Medical Units (MMUs) to extend healthcare access (introduced in 2008). The Mobile Medical Units are there to bring primary healthcare services directly to the doorstep of the population, particularly in remote areas, but they are limited with what they can do owing to difficulties in accessibility.

I smiled when I read about the Mobile Medical Units, and thought of Dad with his own MMU – a clapped-out old Land Rover that kept breaking down and getting stuck in the mud as he endeavoured to get from one end of his practice to the other. He'd already provided testimony that relying on vehicles, particularly during the monsoon, was not necessary a good thing. When I found the following report, I realised that difficulties do still exist on Dufflaghur.

"India's Community Health Workers Were Overworked. Then Came a Pandemic" by Sanskrita Bharadwaj (5 August 2020): Published in Vice Magazine, and written from the perspective of an ASHA worker (Accredited Social Health Activist).

The above states that the ASHA Programme was introduced in 2006 to dispense healthcare to tea gardens in remote and inaccessible regions. ASHA workers have proved indispensable to the healthcare framework of Assam, and are instrumental in making reproductive, maternal and child health care accessible to people in rural areas (tea gardens) and slum clusters of urban areas. However, the report highlights how the workers continue to confront hurdles relating to low pay, inadequate resources and demanding working environments. It specifically refers to the challenges faced by an ASHA worker on Dufflaghur Tea Estate.

It further indicates that transport continues to be a key issue on Dufflaghur, where the ambulance can only be used with the manager's permission. Sometimes the manager does not let the ASHA worker use the ambulance, and at other times, the vehicle is out of service. When someone needs the ambulance, an ASHA has to "shell out" their own money to get a private vehicle to the nearest civil hospital, which is about half an hour away. This money is almost never reimbursed.

The report also highlights that if a delivery requires a C-section, then the patient is referred to a hospital in Tezpur town, which is three-hours away from Dufflaghur. It confirms that Assam now has the highest maternal mortality rate among the Indian states, and this is particularly high in its tea estates. The report then goes on to describe how pressures intensified with the arrival of COVID-19. It does not make for happy reading.

Strangely, the above report was the only reference I could find to Dufflaghur Tea Estate, but I did find another one covering medical conditions on a block of tea gardens (Dhekiajuli Block) in upper Assam.

"The Situation of the Assam Tea Garden Hospitals and Delivery of Reproductive and Child Health Services: A Study of Dhekiajuli Block, Sonitpur, Assam" by Ms. Suchita Topno, Tata Institute of Social Sciences, Mumbai. (Indian Journal of Health Social Work, Jan 2020 Supplement)

"India, as a developing nation, has comparatively more rural than urban areas, and post-independence, the healthcare systems have primarily been focusing on improving the health status of the rural population, by implementing different policies and programs. No doubt the programs and policies have achieved several turning points in the healthcare sector, but the results are not as satisfying when we

see the current maternal mortality rate (MMR), infant mortality rate (IMR) and level of malnutrition in the rural areas. The reason is the lack of skilled human resources, lack of infrastructure, quality of health care services and poor implementation of the services and accessibility."

Ms Topno goes on to say that only a few of the tea garden hospitals are actually functional, with relatively few having a full-time medical officer. The others either have a visiting medical officer, or no doctors at all. Her studies reveal that overall, the quality of the tea garden hospitals is low, and the community health workers face immense challenges.

She continues:

"...though the State Government implemented different schemes and programs, like bringing tea gardens under the Public-Private-Partnership (PPP) Model and introducing the Mobile Medical Unit (MMU) under National Health Mission, the health status hasn't improved much."

The report highlights the following disturbing points:

1. The hospitals are in a pathetic condition.
2. The location of tea gardens has a major impact on the implementation of any scheme or programme.
3. The tea gardens nearer to the Dhekiajuli town had comparatively better health status over the remote ones.
4. The rate of anaemic girls is still rising, impacting maternal health during pregnancy and post-delivery.
5. Most of the tea garden authorities do not prioritise health, considering this to be of secondary importance.
6. Irregular and insufficient drug supply, poor ambulance service and non- functional MMUs add to the burden.
7. Although the State Government has introduced special schemes and programmes (Wage Compensation Schemes, Free Drug Scheme, PPP, etc), there is still a huge gap in terms of implementation, lack of proper monitoring and evaluation of the health system, poor infrastructure and shortage in medical equipment and human resources.
8. Malnutrition is increasingly high.

9. Due to the large and scattered geographical area of the tea gardens in the Dhekiajuli blocks, the community health workers, especially the ASHAs, face a lot of problems in providing health care services to the people.
10. Since the conditions of the hospitals are pathetic, only vaccinations can be given. Other facilities cannot be used.
11. It was found that although women in the tea gardens have submitted the required documents for wage compensation schemes, launched in 2019, no one (to the date of this report) has received financial assistance.
12. Under the PPP model, it was promised that the infrastructure of the tea garden hospitals would be improved and skilled professionals would be recruited, but the conditions of the tea garden hospitals are still poor.
13. It was found that among the 15 tea gardens, there were 7 doctors available, others have visiting doctors, or no doctors at all, and only two tea gardens have doctors with MBBS degree.
14. The ASHA workers are not equally distributed in the tea gardens. In some, there are no ASHA workers at all.
15. Although healthcare in the developing areas of Assam is better, the situation in the tea gardens has not improved much.

This was disappointing – as was a third report, published by *News Click* on 12 January 2022.

"Home to Large Tea Estates, Assam's Behali Still Lacks Sufficient Healthcare Facilities" by Sandipan Talukdar (12 January 2022)

This report states that Behali houses the largest tea garden of Assam: Monabarie Tea Estate, which is owned by McLeod Russel (part of the Williamson Magor Group). There are also a number of other tea gardens, including: Borgang Tea Estate (owned by Goodricke) and Behali Tea Estate (under Williamson Magor).

It goes on to describe the same type of issues as those illustrated in the earlier reports, and highlights the fact that healthcare facilities in Behali remain deficient in meeting the basic needs of patients.

When I finally came upon reports (2015) by Justin Rowlatt for the BBC (*The Bitter Story Behind the UK's National Drink*; *The Real Cost of a Cuppa*; and *Reporter "Trapped" on Indian Tea Plantation*), I felt I'd been suitably provided with a good overview and visual testimony of current conditions (medical and general) prevailing on many tea gardens in Assam – particularly the remote ones.

New Initiatives

From all these accounts, it seemed that nothing had improved regarding medical services for remote tea gardens in the seventy years since my parents were in Assam; but as I searched further, I was interested to find a more recent article in the *Assam Times*, by Shajid Khan (independent journalist based in Assam), dated 23 January 2025.

"Assam to Upgrade Tea Garden Hospitals into Ayushman Aarogya Mandir Sub-Centres"

"In a landmark move to enhance healthcare access for tea garden workers, the Assam state health department has announced a plan to upgrade tea garden hospitals into Ayushman Aarogya Mandir Sub-Centres. The initiative, part of the government's broader strategy to improve healthcare infrastructure in underserved regions, was formalized through multiple agreements, signed this week. Health and Family Welfare Minister, Ashok Singhal, presided over the signing ceremony held at Janata Bhawan in Dispur. The agreement, signed with tea garden management representatives, outlines plans to transform existing tea garden hospitals into fully equipped sub-centres. The upgraded facilities will provide essential medical services, including free diagnostic services and essential drugs,

ensuring accessible healthcare for tea garden workers and their families.

"Simultaneously, the district administration in Udalguri took a significant step by signing a Memorandum of Understanding (MoU) with representatives from 23 tea gardens. Led by Additional District Commissioner, Sarfaraz Haque, the agreement was signed at the District Commissioner's office. Under this MoU, 25 tea garden hospitals in Udalguri will be upgraded to Ayushman Aarogya Mandir Sub-Centres. Speaking at the event, Minister Ashok Singhal emphasized the government's commitment to bridging healthcare gaps in the tea garden community. 'This initiative is a vital step toward ensuring equitable healthcare access for tea garden workers and their families,' he stated.

"The upgraded sub-centres will be equipped with modern healthcare amenities, aiming to address long-standing healthcare challenges faced by the tea garden population. The initiative is expected to improve overall health outcomes and reduce the healthcare inequities experienced by these communities. With this development, Assam continues its efforts to strengthen healthcare delivery, reaffirming its commitment to the welfare of the tea garden workforce, a crucial pillar of the state's economy."

The Future

This certainly seems a promising bit of news. It also accords with what my father tried to do so many times. He never got his upgraded hospital and maternity units with proper facilities. Nor did he get his laboratory. He clearly envisioned what was required all those years ago, but found he was banging his head against a brick wall. Now with the focus, apparently, on upgraded sub-centres with modern healthcare amenities, let's hope this will encourage those in charge to listen and finally do the right thing.

APPENDICES

Dad's Reports

A Note on "Asian" Influenza in Assam (*page 232*)
Malaria Control in a Tea Estate Practice in Assam (*page 235*)
The Infant Parasite Rate on Some Assam Tea Estates (*page 241*)

A Note on "Asian" Influenza in Assam

By ALLAN SCOTT *Chief Medical Officer to a Group of Tea Estates*

This paper has been prepared to demonstrate the highly explosive nature of a recent epidemic of influenza, which is thought to have been the result of infection with virus A/Asia/57.

Because of the clinical nature of the diagnosis and the difficulty in some cases of differentiating clearly between the various forms of acute respiratory infection, especially among children, it has been customary for estates in this practice to graph the weekly new cases of acute respiratory infection in a single group. This group includes coryza, influenza, acute bronchitis, various forms of pneumonia etc., but does not include measles, whooping cough or pulmonary tuberculosis (so far as we are aware).

The appended graphs show the weekly incidence on estates "A" and " B " during 1957 of new cases of acute respiratory infection (as defined above) and of new cases of illness from all causes. The time lost through illness as reflected in the average daily sick from all causes (new and old cases) has been superimposed on the graphs. Two statistical fallacies must be kept in mind. It is convenient and customary for a mother attending with two sick children to be recorded as one case, unless one or both are sufficiently ill to require in-patient treatment; in the latter circumstances the cases are recorded separately. If any patient has resumed work and again falls ill, he or she

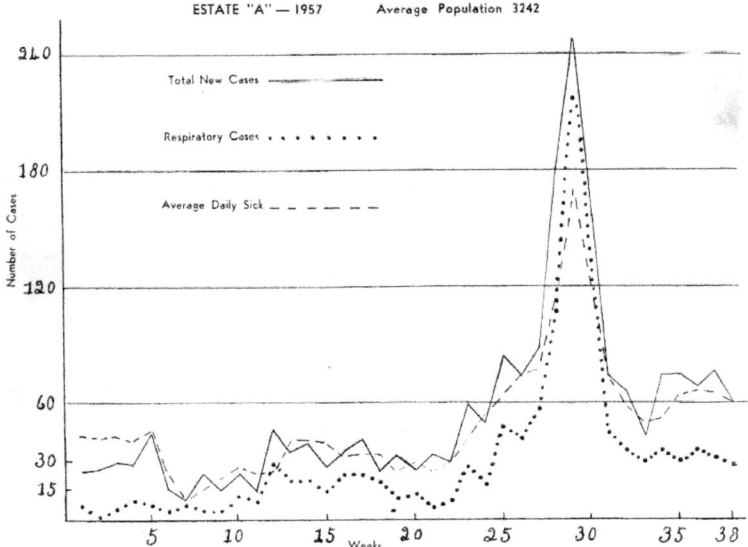

TABLE I. MORBIDITY RATES FOR ESTATES "A" AND "B" DURING THE PERIOD OF EPIDEMIC INCIDENCE OF INFLUENZA IN 1957.

Week No.		25	26	27	28	29	30	31	32	33	34
Weekly new cases of Acute Respiratory Infection as a percentage of estate population	Estate "A"	1.5	1.3	1.7	3.3	6.8	4.0	1.5	1.2	0.9	1.2
	Estate "B"	0.9	0.5	1.1	1.6	2.2	4.5	5.6	3.8	1.1	1.1
Weekly new cases of illness of all types as a percentage of estate population	Estate "A"	2.6	2.3	2.8	5.6	7.7	4.8	2.3	2.0	1.4	2.3
	Estate "B"	2.6	2.0	2.5	3.3	3.8	6.0	6.9	4.8	2.0	2.8
Average daily sick from all causes (new and old cases) as a percentage of estate population	Estate "A"	2.0	2.3	2.3	3.5	5.2	4.1	2.3	1.8	1.5	1.6
	Estate "B"	2.2	2.5	2.5	3.0	4.1	5.2	6.7	5.9	3.3	3.2

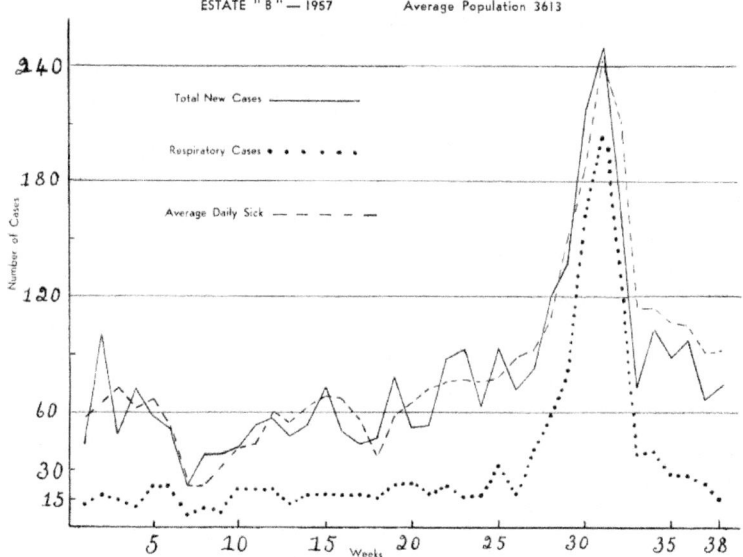

would again be recorded as a new case; however, the number of relapse cases, so far as acute respiratory infection is concerned, has amounted to a very small part of the total.

The typical case of influenza has been mild, with pyrexia for two to four days and incapacity for less than a week. No adverse effect has been noticeable in the vital statistics.

On estate "A" during the seven weeks peak period (weeks 25 to 31), a total of 624 cases of acute respiratory infection were treated and, of these, 618 were recorded as influenza; for the year to date (i.e. weeks 1 to 38 inclusive) the figures are 1,196 and 840 respectively. On estate " B " during the six weeks peak period (weeks 28 to 33) a total of 681 cases of acute respiratory infection were treated and, of these, 566 were recorded as influenza; for the year to date (i.e. weeks 1 to 38 inclusive) the figures are 1,494 and 1,108 respectively.

Table I shows, during the peak period, the morbidity rates as a percentage of the population. Within three weeks (weeks 28 to 30) no less than 14·1% of the population on estate "A" contracted acute respiratory infection, leaving a total of 4·0% of estate population who suffered from all other forms of illness during the same period. On estate " B " during the three weeks (weeks 30 to 32) the figures were 13·9% and 3·8% respectively. On estate "A" for the year to date, children have amounted to well over 50% of the recorded cases of acute respiratory infection; on estate " B," during the same period, the figure was a little under 50%.

During week 29 on estate "A" and week 31 on estate " B " the average daily sick from all causes (new and old cases) reached 5·2% and 6·7% of estate population. Because illness among children normally entails the mother's absence from work for ancillary nursing duties, the excessive rate of sickness gave great cause for concern for a few weeks. The epidemic disappeared, however, as dramatically as it had started.

I wish to acknowledge thanks to the assistant medical officers and other hospital personnel whose careful routine records make a paper of this nature possible.

Malaria Control in a Tea Estate Practice in Assam

By ALAN SCOTT
Principal Medical Officer

Reprinted from the JOURNAL OF TROPICAL MEDICINE AND HYGIENE, *November, 1958*

Malaria Control in a Tea Estate Practice in Assam

By ALAN SCOTT

Principal Medical Officer

The practice to be discussed consists of twelve tea estates and a total resident population (workers and dependants) of 28,000, and is spread out against the Himalayan foothills, north of the Brahmaputra River in the Assam Valley, as shown roughly in the appended map. In the areas intervening between tea estates the main pre-occupation of the relatively scanty rural population is rice cultivation.

Malaria transmission is seasonal, starting about the beginning of April and ending in the latter half of October. The important vector is *Anopheles minimus*. Prior to 1947 malaria control was confined mainly to clearing vegetation from streams and drains, some shading, and a variable amount of larvicidal oil spraying to proved or potential breeding places of the vector.

Chemo-prophylaxis on an extensive scale was introduced in 1947. From the beginning of April that year mepacrine was administered in a dosage which varied between 0·1 G and 0·2 G twice weekly, to the adult working population only. Daily administration of the drug was not attempted. Towards the end of September, 1947, mepacrine was replaced by proguanil in a dosage of 0·1 G twice weekly to all adults, and to children in proportionately reduced dosage, until the end of October. From 1948 proguanil prophylaxis in bi-weekly dosage remained unchanged until the introduction of the 0·3 G tablet in 1950, when the adult dose was changed to 0·3 G once weekly, with a proportionately reduced dose once weekly to children, from April to October inclusive, each year. In 1951, which was rather exceptional, five of the twelve estates tried to withhold chemo-prophylaxis for adults, but continued with the usual dosage of proguanil once weekly for children. By the middle of July two of these estates were forced by rising malaria incidence to start urgent proguanil administration once weekly to adults. In 1953 the adult dose of proguanil was reduced from 0·3 G to 0·15 G (half a large tablet) once weekly and three estates administered mepacrine prophylaxis to adults. The weekly proguanil administration to children remained unchanged on all estates. In 1954 an effort was made to discontinue chemo-prophylaxis in favour of vector control, but for reasons to be discussed later, it became necessary to introduce urgent drug prophylaxis (mainly proguanil) on several estates during the latter half of the transmission season. Since 1954, however, no chemo-prophylaxis has been used at all.

The annual consumption of mepacrine and proguanil during the period 1945-57 is shown in Table I. It has been impossible to separate the drugs into quantities used for chemo-prophylaxis and quantities used for the treatment of clinical malaria, the figures given being the total for all purposes. Neither chloroquine, amodiaquine, pyrimethamine nor quinine has ever been used for prophylactic purposes.

Although some residual insecticide spraying with 50% DDT, W.W.P., and 6·5% gamma BHC, W.D.P., had been carried out from 1947 and 1951 respectively, it was not until 1954 that an effort was made to concentrate on residual insecticide spraying with gamma BHC as the sole method of malaria control. This, however, was fraught with unforeseen difficulties. The suppliers were unable to meet the demand for BHC in full and a considerable proportion of that which became available was held up by a bottle-neck in the river communications. Rising malaria rates, as shown in the graph, necessitated the urgent introduction of chemo-prophylactic drugs on several estates. Although consumption of 6·5% gamma BHC, W.D.P. for the year, as shown in Table I, eventually reached nearly 20,000 lbs., this was applied

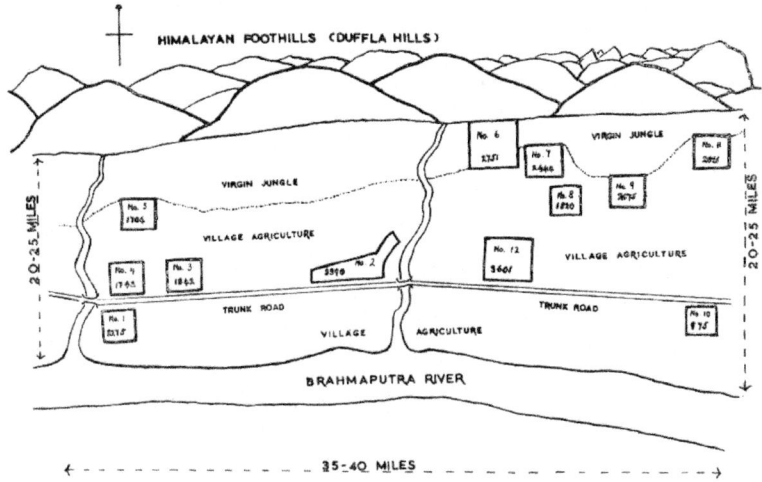

The number and population of each estate are given, and all are less than 500 feet above sea level.

ROUGH MAP OF THE PRACTICE.

mainly during the second half of the transmission season, after a considerable amount of malaria transmission had already taken place. This was in contradistinction to the position during 1953, when the annual consumption of 6·5% gamma BHC, W.D.P., although amounting to less than 9,000 lbs., was applied mainly in the first half of the transmission season.

Since 1955 residual insecticide spraying with 6·5% gamma BHC, W.D.P., has been the only method of malaria control in use and the total annual consumption, as shown in Table I, has shown little cause for concern. The aim has been to apply gamma BHC at the rate of

TABLE I. ANNUAL CONSUMPTION OF SUBSTANCES USED FOR THE CONTROL OF MALARIA IN THE PRACTICE 1945–1957

Year	Mepacrine 0·1 G tablets	Proguanil 0·1 G tablets	Proguanil 0·3 G tablets	Pounds of DDT 50% W.W.P.	Pounds of 6·5% Gamma BHC, W.D.P.
1945	19,286	Nil	Nil	Nil	Nil
1946	95,464	Nil	Nil	Nil	Nil
1947	596,211	181,294	Nil	470	Nil
1948	79,400	1,152,594	Nil	3,844	Nil
1949	50,040	1,125,329	60,000	5,286	Nil
1950	41,260	533,291	367,000	6,318	Nil
1951	45,300	310,800	325,950	2,674	4,120
1952	2,650	160,600	512,451	790	7,014
1953	229,093	153,770	239,333	640	8,897
1954	20,216	56,030	120,318	498	19,952
1955	1,000*	28,592*	93,454*	56	29,479
1956	900	15,102	53,903	14	32,412
1957	4,920	15,525	35,881	148	33,581

*For clinical purposes only, after 1954.

10 mgm. per square foot to potential indoor resting places of *Anopheles minimus*, at intervals of four-five weeks in the first half of the season (March to June) and at intervals of six-seven weeks in the second half of the season (July to September), making a total of five, six or very occasionally seven rounds of spraying for the year. The last round of spraying has frequently been at the rate of 5·0 mgm. per square foot, making a total of 50 – 65 mgm. per square foot for the year. It should be remembered, however, that the accuracy of the rates of application quoted above inevitably depends on the accuracy of the estimates of internal surface area, which in our experience have been notoriously easy to underestimate. With this in mind we have made a point of keeping the consumption (in gallons) of gamma BHC water dispersion high during the first half of the season (March to June), so that some 70 – 75% of annual BHC consumption has already been applied before the end of June, by which time the main monsoon, starting about the middle of the month, has already become well established. The surface area estimates on which we have worked have averaged between 1,500 square feet and 2,500 square feet per household unit. The household unit according to our definition, includes dwelling house, cattle sheds and any other outhouses, all of which usually consist of thatch roofs and mud plaster walls. Completion of the first round of spraying before the onset of the transmission season (i.e. before the end of March) is considered by us to be very important. Whether the daily issue of water dispersible powder has been weighed, or measured by the inevitable cigarette tin, a thorough check on the percentage error of measurement, calculated from the quantities left in stock at the end of each round, has frequently revealed the application to be considerably lighter than the daily measurement calculation has suggested. Since 1956, villages adjacent to several estates have been included in the routine spraying programme. It is felt that this has had a potent effect on the results obtained.

Table II shows the morbidity rates for the practice during the period 1945-57. From 561 in 1945 the malaria rate per mille dropped to 283 with the introduction of incomplete mass chemo-prophylaxis in 1947. By the time non-workers and children had been absorbed into the scheme in 1948 the malaria rate per mille fell rapidly to 66. From this level the rate has declined fairly steadily and the changeover in 1955 to gamma BHC as the sole method of malaria control has seen further improvement,

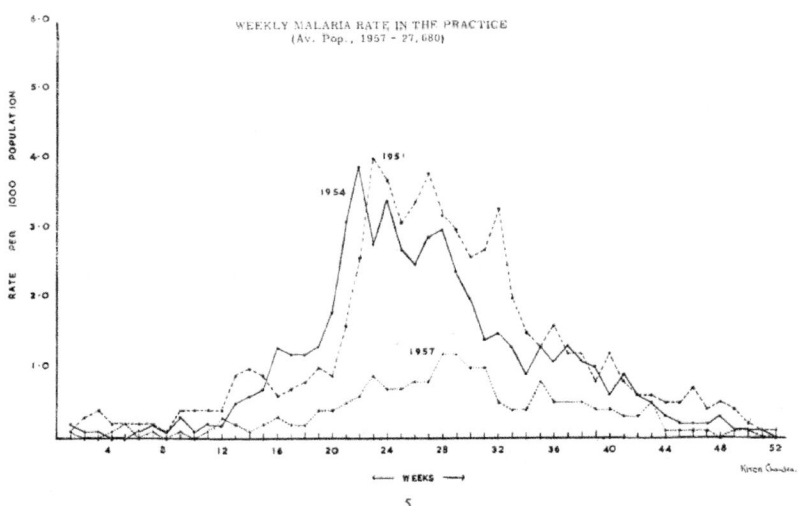

the rate in 1957 at 18 being the lowest ever recorded. Statistical records for the war years are incomplete. In 1938 and 1939, however, the malaria rates per mille for the practice were 548 and 506 respectively. From 49·2% in 1946 the "cold weather spleen rate" of children aged 1–12 years has decreased to 0·4% in 1957. Of the 5,914 children examined in December, 1957, only 24 had palpable spleens. Of those 24 children, eight (33%) had also been picked out at the muster in the previous year and three were children of labourers recruited during 1957. Only one of the remaining 13 children was less than five years old. This was a girl aged three years. Four out of twelve estates recorded nil spleen rates. This is in striking contrast to practice averages of 65·2% and 51·6% recorded in 1938 and 1939. The pre-war and post-war spleen rates for individual estates are shown in Table III. Estate No. 1, situated in open country near the bank of the Brahmaputra River, has never had high spleen rates. Most of the other estates, on the other hand, are situated in the seepage belt against foothills and jungle and some of the latter have had very high spleen rates in the past. The figure of 93·0% on Estate No. 12 for the year 1938 was recorded by Dr. G. C. Ramsay, former principal of the India Branch of the Ross Institute of Tropical Hygiene.

The influence of malaria control as one of many factors affecting the total sick from all causes (new case morbidity rate) is shown in Table II. The rate per mille has dropped from 2,078 in 1945 to 1,094 in 1957. The figures recorded in 1938 and 1939 were 2,107 and 2,077 respectively. The time lost through illness as reflected in the average daily sick from all causes (new and old cases) per mille has decreased from 37·8 in 1945 to 19·4 in 1957. The corresponding figures for the peak period May to October, inclusive, were 42·4 in 1946 and 25·6 in 1957. Of the available records July 1946 and July 1950 are the only two months during which the average daily sick from all causes reached 5% of population. In 1945, however, Estate No. 8 individually recorded devastating average daily sick rates of 6·9%, 8·4%, 11·7%, 9·7%, 7·8% and 9·8% for the period May to October inclusive.

The vital statistics for the practice are shown in Table IV. From 22,400 in 1946 the population, which is almost entirely recruited from other parts of India, has increased to 27,680 in 1957. Because of the constant recruitment and repatriation which has gone on in varying degree each year until only two or three years ago, the age structure of the population has remained artificial, in so far as children and young adults constitute a very high proportion of the population. The results of this are readily seen in the birth and crude death rates, at 43·1 and 10·5 per mille, respectively, in 1957. For the period 1941–45 the average annual crude death rate works out at 25·8 per mille. With the more settled population of to-day it is hoped that the birth rate may start to decline as the artificiality of the age grouping of the population becomes less marked, if for no other reason. The medical and social advancement of

TABLE II. MORBIDITY RATES FOR THE PRACTICE 1945–1957

Year	Average Population	Total new cases from all causes		Malaria		"Cold Weather Spleen Rate" of Children (1–12 years)
		No. of cases	Rate per Mille	No. of cases	Rate per Mille	
1945[1]	18,772	39,002	2,078	10,534	561	N.K.
1946	22,400	42,451	1,895	10,374	463	49·2%
1947	23,506	40,422	1,720	6,658	283	19·3%
1948	23,892	37,480	1,569	1,572	66	N.K.
1949	24,909	40,335	1,619	1,619	65	10·0%
1950	24,974	38,367	1,536	1,145	46	8·7%
1951	25,484	34,405	1,351	1,619	64	4·9%
1952	25,936	32,894	1,268	1,160	45	4·1%
1953	25,229	27,999	1,110	898	36	2·3%
1954	25,965	32,399	1,247	1,397	54	2·1%
1955	27,227	31,247	1,148	981	36	1·3%
1956	27,410	30,963	1,130	618	23	1·1%
1957[2]	27,680	30,270	1,094	493	18	0·4%

[1] No figures were available for two estates in 1945.
[2] One estate (No. 8) was closed for four weeks (23-6-57 to 20-7-57).
The statistical error for 1957 is between 0·5% and 1·0% for the morbidity figures.

TABLE III. INDIVIDUAL "COLD WEATHER SPLEEN RATES" OF CHILDREN (1–12 YEARS) PER CENT. ESTATES No. 1 to 12.

Year	No. 1	No. 2	No. 3	No. 4	No. 5	No. 6	No. 7	No. 8	No. 9	No. 10	No. 11	No. 12	Practice Average
1938	17·8	65·1	59·0	62·0	87·8	69·8	73·5	70·0	57·0	48·7	76·4	93·0	65·2
1939	11·8	43·4	48·8	–	70·2	63·4	59·6	62·5	57·2	–	67·4	55·1	51·6
1946	10·0	63·5	36·4	42·2	58·0	74·9	65·4	49·5	56·0	60·5	37·0	46·6	49·2
1947	2·8	15·4	15·2	11·0	56·9	26·2	14·0	27·1	43·0	28·9	12·0	9·5	19·3
1956	0·0	0·7	0·3	0·4	2·2	1·6	0·3	1·8	1·7	2·0	2·9	0·1	1·1
1957	0·3	0·3	0·2	0·0	0·9	0·8	0·2	0·0	0·0	0·0	1·3	0·2	0·4

Estates No. 4 and No. 6 recorded rates of 75% and 85% respectively, in 1935.
Estate No. 8 recorded a rate of 75% in 1936.

TABLE IV. VITAL STATISTICS FOR THE PRACTICE 1946–1957.

Year	Average total population	Birth rate per 1000 population	Crude death rate per 1000 population	Infant mortality per 1000 live births	Neonatal mortality per 1000 live births
1946	22,400	41·5	19·7	146·4	77·5
1947	23,506	39·7	18·2	140·4	71·8
1948	23,892	49·6	17·8	111·3	70·0
1949	24,909	48·3	19·9	124·0	70·7
1950	24,974	45·0	17·2	96·1	54·3
1951	25,484	44·3	16·9	92·0	57·5
1952	25,936	46·2	13·0	81·0	50·9
1953	25,229	47·6	13·9	78·2	46·6
1954	25,965	42·1	14·8	98·8	65·9
1955	27,227	49·7	12·5	65·0	44·3
1956	27,410	48·0	11·0	65·3	37·2
1957	27,680	43·1	10·5	57·8	27·6

the community, as reflected in the infant mortality rate, has shown substantial improvement during the period under review. From 146·4 in 1946 and 151·3 in the period 1941–45, the infant mortality rate per 1,000 live births has dropped steadily to 57·8 in 1957. With a reduction in the neonatal mortality rate per 1,000 live births from 77·5 in 1946 to 27·6 in 1957, it would appear that pregnant women are now better able to produce sturdy infants than they were several years ago. One wonders whether the high neonatal mortality associated with poor malaria control in 1954 was co-incidental or not.

Summary and Conclusions

The anti-larval, mass chemo-prophylactic and anti-adult phases of malaria control in a tea estate practice in Assam are briefly described. The thoroughly satisfactory nature of gamma BHC as a residual insecticide under the conditions prevailing locally, is demonstrated.

Acknowledgements

I wish to acknowledge my gratitude to Dr. A. B. Gilroy, Principal of the India Branch of the Ross Institute of Tropical Hygiene, for advice and technical guidance, and to Dr. J. Hay Arthur, Chief Medical Officer, Bhatpara Central Hospital, Kalchini, West Bengal, for advice and demonstration of his statistical methods.

References

BARLOW, F., and HADAWAY, A. B. (1956), Nature (correspondence) clxxviii, 1299.
GILROY, A. B. (1951), Ind. J. Mal., v, 2.
―― (1952a), Ann trop. Med. Parasit., xlvi, 72.
―― (1952b), Ibid, xlvi, 121.
HADAWAY, A. B. (1956), Bull. Wld. Hlth. Org., xiv, 813.
MUIRHEAD-THOMPSON, R. C. (1949), Nature, clxiii, 109.
VISWANATHAN, D. K., BHATIA, S. C., and HALGERI, A. V. (1955), Ind. J. Mal., ix, 51.

Indian Journal of Malariology, **12**, 3, September 1958.

THE INFANT PARASITE RATE ON SOME ASSAM TEA ESTATES.

BY

A. B. GILROY,

(*Principal, Ross Institute of Tropical Hygiene, India Branch.*)

AND

A. SCOTT.

(*Medical Officer, Bishnauth Medical Association.*)

[May 17, 1958.]

INTRODUCTION.

In 1957, the infant parasite rate was used to measure the amount of malaria transmission that might still be taking place on a group of Assam tea estates whose malaria morbidity and spleen rates, already low, were steadily falling.

This planting district lies north of the Brahmaputra River, and close to the foot-hills of the North East Frontier Agency. The resident population of the group numbered 27,680 in 1957 and included about 6,000 children aged between two and nine years. Applying the 1956 birth rate of 48 per mille, the expected number of infants would be about 1,300.

The malaria vector is *Anopheles minimus* and the transmission season lasts from April to October or early November.

MALARIA CONTROL.

In 1947 mepacrine was given as a mass suppressive; in 1948 it was replaced by proguanil in a dosage of 100 mg. twice weekly at first, and 300 mg. once weekly later.

D.D.T. was first used in 1948 but was soon replaced by B.H.C. which, after 1954, was the sole method of malaria control. The insecticide regime was to apply a concentration of 10 mg. per square foot (110 mg. per square metre) from March to October with intervals of six weeks between rounds.

Though house spraying in the early years was neither as efficient nor as effective as it became later, yet together with mass-suppressives it resulted in an immediate and dramatic fall in the morbidity and spleen rates.

MALARIA INDICES.

Table I refers to the medical practice of 12 estates from which nine were selected for the infant parasite rate investigation.

In 1946, the morbidity rate was 463 per mille and the spleen rate in children aged two to nine years was 49 per cent.

1947 reflected the first year of control by a morbidity rate almost halved and a spleen rate more than halved. In 1948, further substantial reductions were obtained. Thereafter until 1951, the morbidity rate was fairly stationary though the spleen rate continued to fall each year. After 1954, when B.H.C. replaced D.D.T., the decrease in malaria morbidity was steady (except for a rise in 1954) and by 1957 the rate had fallen to 18 per mille.

TABLE I.

Annual malaria morbidity and spleen rates.

Year	Average population	Malaria cases per mille	Spleen rate per cent
1946	22,400	463	49·2
1947	23,506	283	19·3
1948	23,892	66	—*
1949	24,904	65	10·0
1950	24,974	46	8·7
1951	25,484	64	4·9
1952	25,936	45	4·1
1953	25,229	36	2·3
1954	25,965	54	2·1
1955	27,227	36	1·3
1956	27,410	23	1·1
1957	27,680	18	0·4

*Not recorded.

THE SPLEEN RATE.

As early as 1951 the spleen rate had fallen to five per cent and by 1957, to 0·4 per cent, only 24 of 5,914 children examined having palpable spleens. As it approached zero the spleen rate was no longer a guide to malaria morbidity;

thus a spleen rate of 8·7 per cent in 1950 was associated with a morbidity rate of 46 per mille, while in 1952, though the morbidity rate was unchanged, the spleen rate had fallen to 4·1 per cent.

THE INFANT PARASITE RATE.

Infants born between January 1 and June 30, 1957 were examined fortnightly by thick and thin blood smears. It was realised that examinations starting in the first week of July were too late and that infections early in the transmission season would be missed. Unfortunately, other commitments prevented an earlier start.

Although a few mothers refused permission, it was possible to start the series with 333 infants, all but five of whom completed the tests. Two of these departed with their parents from the district, and three died (the causes of death were recorded as congenital debility, dysentery and pneumonia).

Since the estates are surrounded by villages where there is no malaria control whatever, it was necessary to keep a careful watch for infants who spent one or more nights away from their homes. Altogether 47 infants had to be excluded because of such absences, leaving 286 who never left the estates and who had blood smears taken fortnightly from the beginning of July to the beginning of November.

Of the 286, 14 were infected with malaria (Table II) giving a parasite rate of 4·9 per cent. None of the 14 was positive on more than one fortnightly examination.

TABLE II.

Species of malaria parasites.

Species	Form	Number of infants
P. falciparum	Trophozoites.	5
	Gametocytes.	3
P. vivax	Trophozoites.	2
	Trophozoites and gametocytes.	2
	Gametocytes.	1
P. malariae	Gametocytes.	1
		14

The dates of finding positive blood smears are given in Table III. As three infants were positive at the first examination, it is more than likely that a number of earlier infections were missed and that the rate throughout the full transmission season would have been considerably higher than 4·9 per cent.

Of the 14 infants positive for malaria, 11 were infected up to August and only three afterwards.

Five of these infants lived on one estate and the remaining nine were distributed between five estates. This is shown in Table IV.

TABLE III.

Dates when blood was positive for malaria parasites.

Week ending	Number of infants positive
1957 July 13	3
July 27	1
August 3	2
August 10	2
August 24	3
September 7	1
September 21	1
September 26	1
	14

TABLE IV.

Places of residence of infants.

Estate	Number of infants completing test	Number positive for malaria
A	28	1
B	39	1
C	42	5
D	19	2
E	13	Nil
F	37	Nil
I	27	3
K	36	2
L	45	Nil
	286	14

The numbers of infants on each estate are too small to establish with any confidence, imperfections in a residual insecticide regime supposedly uniform on all estates. Estate C is a possible exception although the malaria morbidity for the year, 9·8 per mille, was only half the rate for the group and the spleen rate was 0·2 per cent compared with 0·4 per cent for the group.

CONCLUSIONS.

In this group of estates in 1957, a child spleen rate of 0·4 per cent and a malaria morbidity rate at all ages of 18 per mille per annum indicated very satisfactory malaria control following five years of intensive house spraying with B.H.C. Yet 4·9 per cent of 286 infants were infected with malaria during part only of the transmission season.

The persistence of malaria must, in large part, be attributed to uncontrolled villages close to estate boundaries and it is evident that while malaria control in limited areas can be highly successful, eradication is not possible.

In a malaria eradication programme, no reliance can be placed on the spleen rate, however low, as an indication of the degree of residual transmission and only a zero rate is acceptable.

SUMMARY.

Blood examination of infants on a group of tea estates in Assam showed that there was still a considerable amount of malaria transmission despite low morbidity and spleen rates.

Of 286 infants, 14 were infected with malaria between June and November, 1957.

In this year, the malaria morbidity rate at all ages was 18 per mille and the child spleen rate was 0·4 per cent.

ABOUT THE AUTHOR

The author was born in Glasgow, but was brought up in Kent. She studied languages, then moved to France to work as a secretary, first with Campanile, then with Interpol. When she returned to the UK, she joined Strathclyde Police (now Police Scotland). On retiring from the police, she studied creative writing at Glasgow University and pursued an interest in Spiritualism and Psychical Research. In 2020, she became President of the Glasgow Association of Spiritualists, and retired from this position in 2024. *The Assam Diaries: Medicine on a Tropical Tea Estate during the 1950s* is the author's fourth work of non-fiction.

Books by Caroline Allana Scott
(www.writingtoheal.uk)

Spiritualism

Stories of the Pioneers: Mediums, Healers and Psychical Researchers (written as The Glasgow Association of Spiritualists)
God to Malaria: Communications from the Spirit World (written as The Glasgow Association of Spiritualists)
The World of Spirit by P'shanta: Through the Trance Mediumship of Mrs Edith Thomson (written as The Glasgow Association of Spiritualists)

Non-Fiction

The Assam Diaries: Medicine on a Tropical Tea Estate during the 1950s

Fiction

Enemy on the Other Side
A Tea Doctor in Assam (due for publication in 2026)

(Author's royalties go to: *Cancer Research UK*)

Printed in Dunstable, United Kingdom